Mindpowered Singles
Creating Life to the Full

Cresenda Jones

Mindpowered Singles: Creating Life to the Full
© 2022, Cresenda Jones

ISBN: 978-1-953623-91-1. Published in the USA by Illumination Publishers, 6010 Pinecreek Ridge Court, Spring, Texas 77379.

Unless otherwise indicated, all Scripture references are from the Holy Bible, New International Version, copyright ©1973, 1978, 1984, 2011 by Biblica, Inc. Used by permission. All rights reserved worldwide.

Cover design by Roy Appalsamy of Toronto, Canada. Interior layout by Toney Mulhollan.

Our books may be purchased in bulk for promotional, educational and theological training use. Contact Illumination Publishers International at IPinfo@ipibooks.com.

The views or emphasis of the author are her own and do not necessarily reflect the views of Illumination Publishers.

About the author: **Cresenda Jones,** a counselor and life coach, has been a disciple since 1986 in North Carolina, Georgia, Pennsylvania, New Jersey, and Florida churches of Christ. Generational trauma and dysfunction led her to intently seek both spiritual maturity and emotional health. Along the journey, her MA in professional counseling, MBA, and M.Ed. have provided clearer roadmaps and growth. She considers it a privilege to witness growth and miraculous transformations when she facilitates the Time Line Therapy® breakthrough process, discussion groups, and workshops. She is most excited when her clients eliminate toxic emotional residue and limiting beliefs that have held them back, freeing them up for the relationships, life, performance, and success that God has planned. You can reach Cresenda at cresenda@cresendajones.com.

ILLUMINATION PUBLISHERS

www.ipibooks.com

Dedication

This book is dedicated to all the courageous book discussion and support group participants, along with my Time Line Therapy® clients who finished their breakthrough processes. You all have encouraged my soul. You are my heroes! You push past insecurities and fears so that you can be more of what God has planned, in increasing measure. I appreciate your commitment to personal, spiritual, character, and emotional growth. Whether you've participated in Philadelphia, South Jersey, Central Jersey, North Jersey, the Bronx, Brooklyn, Miami, Freeport, Bahamas, Palm Beach, or online...you all continue to be the wind beneath my wings!

—Cresenda Jones

Contents

Contents

Acknowledgments

Most of all, I appreciate and thank God, the giver of all life, grace, hope, wisdom, knowledge, strength, power, and growth. With God, all things are possible! Apart from God, I can do nothing (John 15:5).

I appreciate my friends who gave me feedback on this book—Kenda Moloney and Lori Londagin. Thanks similarly to Allan Cunningham and Barbara Manuputy for their input. I also appreciate Gina Poirier's writing expertise and support for me—the math major! Paul Vasquez and Toney Mulhollan (of Illumination Publishers) work hard to provide resources for what matters most—our spiritual health. I greatly appreciate them both! A special thanks to Kyle Spears for taking time in his busy schedule to write the foreword. His desire to support and encourage others is admirable and heartening.

There are no words that could ever express my deep gratitude for my brothers and sisters who have cohosted with me discussion groups on the *Healing for Damaged Emotions Workbook* (by David Seamands), on my book, *Spiritual Transformation: Emotional Intelligence and Freedom,* and a women's support group: Heather Johnson, Natacha Pierre, Derek Sippio, Bev Ozanne, Doug Johnson, Aaron Tussing, Derek Canton, Gayle Knutson, Crystal Broadbent, Delicia Douglas, Kenda Moloney, Theresa Clark, Wendy Walker-Drakes, Ibironke Cunningham, and Paulette Lozaique. Partnerships on the journey to be all we can be for God are priceless. You all are ahhh-mazing!

And, lastly, I am forever grateful for my mom, Joyce Siler. She has given her continuous support and love. Even as she approaches eighty-three, she is always thinking of how she can be of help. She has given her all to "fight the good fight of the faith" (1 Timothy 6:12).

Foreword

One of the most challenging journeys that many who follow Christ experience is that of singleness. Not only are singles the most diverse group in churches, their needs are also consistently overlooked as we direct our resources toward other ministries. It is my belief that singles need and deserve the same level of quality and expertise that other ministries receive. Singles live deeply complex lives that require a certain level of understanding. If there is a book to address the specific emotional-spiritual needs singles have, this book is the one. It should be a principal read.

As a mental health professional who integrates spirituality, Cresenda addresses emotional-spiritual challenges with clarity. One of the struggles for Christians seeking to address their mental health needs is to continue to be led by the Holy Spirit. There are many wonderful approaches to healing that fall short of helping someone turn to Jesus for the power to heal. It is also hard to find material that doesn't dismiss the real mental health issues plaguing Christ followers everywhere. Cresenda helps readers to skillfully navigate both worlds as they pursue healing.

Although the book is informative, it also provides space for a process to take place. This is especially important for me as a provider, as I regularly give homework to clients between sessions. Insight doesn't automatically lead to change; being able to functionally process is essential. Cresenda wisely builds on her previous framework regarding emotional intelligence. Emotional intelligence is part information and part experiential. In other words, Cresenda helps the reader all the way from assessment to action steps. I believe this is the true power in her book. There are more people seeking help for mental health than ever, but not everyone has access to therapy. This is part of the reason books like this are essential.

In addition to a process-oriented approach, she addresses the deeply complicated aspects that are unique to singleness. One of the trickiest parts of healing to address is how to name the pain or discomfort. Until we can put a name to our experiences, we tend to remain disoriented. Cresenda provides orientation for where singles of all ages and circumstances find themselves. She addresses the rarely discussed issues that singles face and gives permission to fully feel those losses. Furthermore, her own transparency with regard to her own losses is as piercing a testimonial as I've come across in some time. The grief that singles face is part of what adds to the loneliness, and the people of God need a way to functionally lament. Without a trained eye, it is difficult to distinguish when someone has found a healthy way of processing or is instead unaware of the continual cycle that keeps them stuck. Cresenda is aware of the function of what is known as secondary gains and various subconscious mechanisms that remain protected within an individual who has been damaged. There is a plethora of losses in the lives of singles that not only have to be named but also grieved.

One of the most exciting aspects of Cresenda's approach is her understanding of trauma. As a trauma specialist, I evaluate each approach based on the qualities that make it trauma informed. As society embraces mental health, it continues to address how trauma is created in the first place. Cresenda doesn't just understand the basics of being trauma informed, she displays an advanced understanding. I endorse Cresenda's approach, as her material addresses the crux of trauma, our subconscious selves. Trauma injures our inner spirit along with creating rigid associations at a neurological level. A trauma-informed approach takes these important factors into consideration. As a result, we need a specialized approach to fully address how traumatic associations are named and healed. Her attention to detail and understanding of how to create a process result in a viable option for those who have tried other approaches.

Romans 8:28 is an apt scripture that sums up what Cresenda communicates in this book. She helps the reader to embrace the parts of their lives they'd rather not think about, and helps them think the way God thinks about it. She helps to convey that in all things, God is working to teach us more about who we really are and about who he really is. In his infinite wisdom, he has a plan to take us from being a victim to becoming a survivor. Cresenda's book is a survival guide for those who want to go from surviving to thriving.

—Kyle Spears LIMHP, LMFT,
Truth, Trauma, Theology

Introduction

He answered, "Love the Lord your God with all your heart and with all your soul and with all your strength and with all your mind." (Luke 10:27)

"I have come that they may have life, and have it to the full." (John 10:10)

God's promises are not just for the fired-up campus students. God's promises are not only for our teenagers. God's promises are not just for those who have been blessed to be married. God's promises are just as much for those of us who are not married... for those of us who are single. God's promises are for ALL his beloved sons and daughters! His promises are for you and me.

There are many amazing singles written about in the Bible and some who wrote parts of our Bible. We have little trouble believing that God's promises apply to the Apostle Paul, who discussed being content where God has us. In 1 Corinthians 7:7, Paul actually said, "I wish that all of you were as I am. But each of you has your own gift from God; one has this gift, another has that." Paul considered being single to be a *gift*.

We typically don't have issues with believing that God's promises are for someone like Anna (Luke 2:36–38), who was a prophet and single for seventy-seven years after her husband passed. She prayed, fasted, stayed in the temple, and was described as "very old." She lived with her husband for only seven years after their marriage.

It's easy to see God's promises to Mary and Martha. Though Martha was challenged on her focus when Jesus visited her and Mary, it was clear that she mattered to Jesus (Luke 10:38–42).

God's hand in Jeremiah's life is evident despite no mention of him being married. In chapter 16, God even commanded Jeremiah not to marry in that place. Jeremiah recognized God's call (Jeremiah 1:1–9), he trusted that God was in control (17:9), he aligned himself with God's perspective (1:12), constantly prayed (21:2, 29:7, 12, 37:3, 42:2, 4, 20), and allowed others to help him (38:7–13). God trusted Jeremiah, a single man, with his word (1:12).

We have little to no problem understanding that God was working in Ruth's life after she lost so much. Despite deep hurt, shattered dreams, and the desire to marry, she was committed in her faith and to her family while she was single.

We can appreciate God's power in Joseph's life while he was single as he stood the tests of major persecution along with sexual temptations and more trials (Genesis 37–50).

Nehemiah is one of my personal heroes as we see God work mightily in his life despite folks like Sanballat and Tobiah attempting to halt his valiant efforts.

John the Baptist was fierce, impactful, used by God, and was never married (John 3:22–30; Matthew 14:1–12).

Yes, God's promises are meant for you, me, Mary of Magdalene, Martha of Bethany, Mary of Bethany, Miriam, Lydia (Acts 16), Daniel, and all those who never married. Have you forgotten that our Lord and Savior, Jesus, was never married? In a world where marriage is placed on a pedestal and singles are many times treated as if their lives and spirituality matter less than others' who are married, the greatest man who ever walked this earth was single! Jesus is our role model in countless ways. He was a single man for his entire life. He loved and served God completely. He decided that God's will was his own will. Yet in all that he experienced here on earth, he most likely felt many of the emotions that singles can feel—anguished, sad and grief-stricken, desperate, frustrated, provoked, violated, threatened, hurt, disrespected, rejected, overwhelmed, confident, courageous, determined, fulfilled, inspired, joyful, powerful, hopeful, loving, and even peaceful. With God and the Holy Spirit, we can follow in Jesus' footsteps and create our life to the full.

Yes, God's promise of life "to the full" (John 10:10) is for you... no matter whether you have the opportunity to get married or not! None of us knows exactly what God's detailed plans are for our lives, yet when I consider all his promises, how glorious his kingdom is, and how fearfully and wonderfully we each are made, I have no doubt that he is not finished with us yet. God wants us to experience what he has planned—*life to the full*—we just need to choose this life every day, and we can! Just as we have biblical single role models, we too can choose to be role models in this world. We are needed to represent God and his kingdom amidst the spiritual darkness. We are called to be those of salt and light (Matthew 5:13-14) as we live our lives to the full.

In Chapter 1, I share some of my "single yet again" story and how we can walk with God when our dreams are shattered and our hearts feel broken. I discuss John 10:10, one of my favorite scriptures, in Chapter 2. Our priceless spiritual foundation is visited in Chapter 3. In Chapter 4, I share information that we need to understand regarding our brains, mind, and mindpower. In Chapters 5 through 7, I share about being stuck with some harmful and limiting beliefs (after becoming single again) and then about the new decisions we can all choose. Keys to achievable outcomes are also discussed there. Chapter 8 discusses the fact that it will be of no benefit if we gain the entire world yet lose our souls. God's grace in meeting our needs (2 Corinthians 12:8-10) is discussed in Chapter 9. And, lastly, our mind and spiritual power to create life to the full are discussed in Chapters 10 and 11.

REFLECTION

1. Do you believe that God has worked, is working, and will continue to work in your life as a single? How have you seen God's covering and power in your life?

    _____

    _____

    _____

    _____

_____

_____

_____

_____

2. In our world where more respect seems to be given to those who are married, how do you think Jesus, as a single, would be treated today?

_____

_____

_____

_____

_____

_____

_____

_____

3. Does God's John 10:10 plan include you? Does that scripture apply to you? Do you think and feel that it does?

_____

_____

_____

_____

_____

_____

_____

_____

Chapter One

My Story –
Plans for Marriage
...and Then None

*For just as the sky is higher than the earth, so my deeds
are superior to your deeds and my plans superior to your
plans.* (Isaiah 55:9 NET)

*In their hearts humans plan their course, but the LORD
establishes their steps.* (Proverbs 16:9)

I could have titled this chapter "Single Again" since I was
scheduled to get married on Sunday, August 29, 2021. Yes...I was
supposed to get married on a day that sometimes feels like it was
only just a few weeks ago! After thirty-five years of living as a
committed disciple of Jesus, dating a couple of times before this
relationship, and still having the desire for matrimony, I believed
that God had finally answered my prayers for marriage.

I had spent months preparing for our wedding day. The DJ,
photographer, breathtaking oceanfront venue, minister, and Riv-
iera Mayan honeymoon plans were all contracted and confirmed.
I had a great time picking out my wedding dress as about five dear
sister friends and my mom joined me at David's Bridal to select
a dress along with all the accessories. Friends had planned both
a virtual shower and an in-person bridal shower, for those who
lived in close proximity.

My fiancé and I had paid for my dream oceanfront venue and
my beautiful wedding dress. We had deposits down to secure

all the other vendors. I had my two (COVID-19 considerations) bridesmaids, and they had their dresses. If we were not in the midst of a devastating pandemic, I would have had at least five bridesmaids; but with the pandemic, we planned to have only thirty friends at the ceremony and reception party. Yes, after thirty-five years of living as a faithful and sold-out disciple of Christ, it was FINALLY my turn to have a loving and mutually doting partner for my life journey in Christ!

Our story was pretty amazing and seemed like a miraculous answer to prayer. While desiring a husband and family for most of my time as a disciple, many times I felt hopeless regarding the possibility. Due to the pandemic, I moved from in-person book discussion groups to facilitating my first virtual women's discussion group on David Seamands' *Healing for Damaged Emotions Workbook*. The sisters inquired (as usual) about opportunities for their husbands and other brothers in Christ to have the same discussion group. At that time, I had only facilitated one discussion group on Seamands' workbook for brothers, in Miami, Florida. In response to the requests of the married and single sisters, I decided to offer a virtual Men of Freedom discussion group. A sister in the women's group connected me with a brother in Christ who was also a counselor to cohost. In addition, I asked a dear brother friend and partner in the gospel to cohost with us.

At some point it was on my heart yet again to petition God for my long-term dream of marriage. So, a few times, I prayed that my husband would participate in the Men of Freedom II discussion group. I wanted to marry someone who was willing to do their work to be healthy not just spiritually, but also emotionally. Fifty-four brothers signed up to participate in the discussion group. On average, about twenty-five brothers participated in each discussion over thirteen weeks. During the first discussion group on July 18, 2020, there were twenty-seven attendees (including me). We prayed, introduced the cohosts, talked about Romans 12:2, and discussed the guidelines and rationale for the group. Then I shared my story and some statistics about the group of brothers who had signed up. Twenty-six percent had reported that they had a diagnosed or suspected mental health challenge. Anxiety, depression, OCD, PTSD, schizoid personality disorder, dysthymia, ADHD, ADD, and addictions were the reported or suspected diagnoses. That type of information is always encouraging for folks...to know that they are not alone in their challenges.

I had informed the entire group that once we moved into breakouts, if anyone felt uncomfortable with sharing in my presence to just let me know. So that the brothers would feel safe, I didn't want my female presence to be a stumbling block. After giving instructions, we put the twenty-seven participants into triads to discuss the workbook questions. I made note of the breakout group numbers for everyone, in the event that someone had technical difficulties, and then I joined the only breakout group that had two participants. All the other breakout groups had three brothers.

When I joined the breakout group and as we started the discussion, my prayer about a husband was not on my mind. Life had been super busy, as usual. I checked that the two brothers felt comfortable sharing with me in the group, and we talked about the following workbook questions, which are powerful for building deeply connected relationships with anyone:

1. What made you decide to come to this group? Briefly describe what has been happening in your life that makes the topic of *Healing for Damaged Emotions* relevant to your life.

2. What was your family like as you were growing up? How did your parents relate to each other? How did they relate to you? Did you have brothers and sisters? How did you and your siblings get along?

3. Would you describe yourself as a person who is "in touch" with your feelings? Why? What, if any, feelings are difficult for you to express?

4. What would you like to see God do in your life as the result of going through this workbook, *Healing for Damaged Emotions?*

I am not sure at what point the handsome and obviously intelligent disciple mentioned that he was divorced, but I found out that he was single. The other brother in the breakout group was married and living in South Africa. At one point, the South African brother mentioned that he was short. The single brother also said that he was short. So I asked what they meant and how tall they were. My ex-fiancé later told me that when he said he was six feet tall, I actually smiled and clapped my hands. Talk about wearing my subconscious emotions, thoughts, and prayers on my sleeve...I guess that's what I did. Since I am 5 feet 11 inches, my prayer has also included my desire for a husband who is taller than me. The first meeting of Men of Freedom 11 went well, and the participants seemed to be encouraged. I don't recall immediately or consciously thinking that my fellow breakout room participant was an answer to prayer, but I was excited to have met a single brother.

Typically, I ask those in the first discussion breakout group with me to pray for the next group. I contacted the two brothers from the breakout group along with four others for prayer for the following week's discussion. When I contacted my ex-fiancé to request that he pray, we ended up talking for a good amount of time and continued to do so as the days and the discussion group weeks progressed. As we got to know each other, I was impressed with his commitment to God, knowledge of God's word, intelligence, independent thinking, thoughtfulness, service to our country, professionalism, deep work ethic, willingness to do the work to heal, determination, dedication, attention to detail, and acts of service, as wells as the attention he gave to building our friendship. I felt that he was the answer to many of my prayers.

My ex-fiancé is amazing. After he participated in the Men of Freedom 11 group, he was willing to start the Time Line Therapy® breakthrough process to clear out emotional baggage and limiting beliefs. He was the "classic man" I had always prayed for: He had withstood the test of time in God's kingdom after a highly challenging and trauma-producing marriage. As a Marine, he was also the "protection" I had long desired, since I had been sexually assaulted at twelve years old, and our home had been robbed on Christmas day when I was only eight years old. I was totally attracted to him, felt infatuated, and fell deeply in love. It was such a joyful time. In my mind, he was "the perfect package"—the perfect brother for me. I fully thought that he was the answer to my prayers.

We met in person for the first time at the end of August 2020. At the time, I was fifty-three years old and he was fifty-seven. He had been a disciple for twenty years. We started dating officially that October and got engaged in April 2021. As I mentioned, we planned to get married at the end of August 2021. As our plans progressed toward marriage, we found a home that we decided to put an offer on. Though the original plan was for him to move from his state to Florida, he could not find a job and salary that was comparable to his current position. The week in which we planned to finalize our offer to purchase a home in his state, we also had our third or fourth professional pre-marriage counseling session. Throughout our relationship, as with all relationships, we both had some concerns. Fortunately, I stuck to my long-time conviction that if I ever had the opportunity to get married, my fiancé and I would need to get professional pre-marriage counseling in addition to the church's pre-marriage sessions.

Things came to a head or really moved beyond just concerns in our relationship when my fiancé began to consider a promotion at his job. In addition to the other perplexing challenges, this became the straw that broke the camel's back. We talked about his desire for the promotion with our licensed pre-marriage counselor on Monday, July 5, 2021. His job at the time was exceedingly demanding. I just could not wrap my head around my fiancé (at the time) taking on a new job, getting married, learning how to be a godly partner in marriage, buying and renovating a house, moving two households, moving to a different church in his state, building new relationships in the fellowship, and having my mother (who is dealing with dementia) live with us. I really wanted to be married to this amazing man, but it was apparent that his career and our relationship were in too much conflict to move forward. This was a deeply and inexpressibly distressing time.

On Tuesday, July 6, after getting all the contract details from our realtor for an offer on a home, my fiancé and I talked. Because of all our concerns, we decided not to move forward with putting the offer on the house. Despite us both wanting and pushing to move forward, this "put the brakes" on our relationship.

Subsequently, we decided to postpone the wedding. Then at some point in our conversations about our relationship and individual needs, my fiancé asked what all this meant for our relationship. He asked if we were still dating. I said no. Many a time, I have wished I had not said that we were no longer in a relationship. I feel that those decisions were the hardest I have ever had to make. Additional details of our story are not mine to tell, but I really loved and was in love with my fiancé. I believed that if any couple could successfully manage the challenges that presented themselves, we could. Breaking up was beyond heartbreaking, as I was totally invested in our friendship, plans for marriage, and a great future together.

So my engagement story is that we had plans for marriage... and then none. After thirty-five years as a disciple, one dating relationship, and two engagements, I was "single again." After a year of excitement, investment, and planning, this was awfully hard to wrap my head around. I definitely felt that we had combined our lives and that my fiancé was etched on my heart, mind, and soul. Despite the myriad challenges that come with age and lived lives, I was looking forward to our life together. The "withdrawal" was very difficult. It took me about nine months to understand why I was having such a hard time detaching and moving on. I had beliefs and tapes in my mind that became limiting. I had the emotions (stored subconsciously) that come along with any breakup. Among additional reasons, including basic grief, I also realized that it was so hard to detach because my ex-fiancé had become my best friend. That was the end of the relationship, but of course, that is not the end of my personal story. **God always guides us and always provides what we need!**

His divine power has given us everything we need for a godly life through our knowledge of him who called us by his own glory and goodness. (2 Peter 1:3)

Chapter Two

God's Plan for Life to the Full
—John 10:10

I cannot recall exactly when John 10:10 became one of my all-time favorite scriptures. But I do know that I have felt the need to be reminded of God's plan that is laid out in this scripture countless times...especially with the end of the relationship with my ex-fiancé. You'll see that I cite this verse over and over throughout the book! I believe (consciously and subconsciously) that God wants us to have life to the full. You likely know John 10:10 from the NIV: "The thief comes only to steal and kill and destroy; I have come that they may have life, and have it to the full."

After realizing that I needed to align my internal representations (explained in Chapter 5) with God's plan for my life, this scripture came to mind and backed up the learnings I had from the Time Line Therapy® technique used to eliminate negative emotions and limiting beliefs/decisions connected to past events. I needed to decide to create the life to the full that God still had planned for me after becoming single again. God doesn't want us to just "survive" through this life. God has planned for us to thrive!

When studying a particular scripture, I like to look at how it is rendered in different Bible versions. First, it is interesting to note that in all sixty-two versions included on biblegateway.com, "thief" was only translated differently one time. "Robber" was the word used in the New Life Version. Satan, the thief, wants to rob what God has planned for us. In addition, for "the thief comes only," "comes" was also translated as "cometh," "enters," "the thief's purpose is," "is only there to," "comes with the sole intention of," and "approaches with malicious intent." We indeed have a thief—Satan—who is only driven by maliciousness in his intent. We need to be strong in the Lord and in his mighty power (Ephesians 6) in order to stand against the devil's schemes. We need our full armor!

The reality is that we are involved in spiritual warfare. In the NIV, John 10:10 says that Satan, the thief, comes only to **steal and kill and destroy.** Other versions use rob, slaughter, spoil, or slay to describe Satan's intent. Are you aware of Satan's efforts? Can you clearly, with spiritual eyes, see what Satan is attempting to steal or rob? As I grieved the end of my plans for marriage and the end of my relationship with my ex-fiancé, I felt that Satan was doing everything he could to knock me out. I felt his efforts to steal, kill, and destroy my clarity, empowerment, hope, freedom, focus, faithfulness, devotion, self-control, impact, joy, trust in God, identity in God, peace, healthy boundaries, confidence, esteem, agency, serenity, love, patience, kindness, and gentleness. Satan wanted my flesh to kill and destroy the indwelling of God's Spirit (Galatians 5:19–26). Amen that God provides what we need to fight and defeat Satan! And amen for God's amazing grace when we need him in our grief and when we mess up.

The good news is that God has planned life to the full for all his beloved children. To describe this life and why Jesus came to earth, other Bible translations use the following phrases for "life...to the full": more abundantly, have and enjoy life, have it in abundance, live life to the fullest, life in its fullest measure, have it fully, life that is full and good, life in all its fullness, have everything they need, far more life than before, so that they will have everything they need. God is love. God is good. God wants the best for you and me...throughout our entire life and no matter our status (single, married, divorced, engaged, widow, widower, etc.). We are God's beloved sons and daughters.

I also love how Jesus' description of his purpose is translated in the Living Bible version of John 10:10. It notes that, "My purpose is to give life in all its fullness." In addition, The Message seems to always be heartwarming in its translations: "I came so they can have real and eternal life, more and better life than they ever dreamed of."

Since I have no higher education in Bible and ministry, I do not plan to go into exegesis, hermeneutics, or any theological explanations. That's not my wheelhouse. BUT...I do want us to reflect on a few practical questions and applications of John 10:10 in our lives.

REFLECTION

1. Do you really think and feel that John 10:10 includes YOU? Is for YOU? Is about YOU? What three things come to mind when you think about how and where you have seen God bless you with life to the full?

    _____

    _____

    _____

    _____

    _____

    _____

    _____

    _____

2. If, for some reason, you think and feel that John 10:10 applies to everyone but you, have you figured out why you think and feel that way?

    _____

    _____

    _____

    _____

    _____

    _____

    _____

    _____

3. In which areas of your life do you feel you are living the life to the full that God has planned? See the six components of our lives in the circular figure—professional, financial, physical wellness, spiritual, emotional, and relationships. Ranking each area on a scale of 0–10 can be helpful. For a visual, create a spider web (or radar chart) of your rankings.

_____

_____

_____

_____

_____

_____

_____

4. What can you daily thank God for regarding how he has blessed you with a life to the full?

_____

_____

_____

_____

_____

_____

5. In which areas of your life do you feel you need to invest additional attention in order to live life "to the full"—where God is glorified and your spiritual values are realized?

_____

_____

_____

_____

_____

_____

6. Which area that needs attention is most important and urgent? What can you do today, this week, and this month to move you closer to living life to the full in your chosen area?

_____

_____

_____

_____

_____

_____

Chapter Three

Spiritual Foundation

In him was life, and that life was the light of all mankind.
The light shines in the darkness, and the darkness has not
overcome it. (John 1:4–5)

I talked in detail about the importance of a biblical and spiritual foundation in my first book, *Spiritual Maturity: God's Will for Emotional Health and Healing* (available at www.cresendajones. com). In consideration of Mark 8:36, "What good is it for someone to gain the whole world, yet forfeit their soul?" we must always keep in mind that **our relationship with God and the salvation of our souls are our absolute priorities.** These are God's first priorities. All our work toward creating the life God has planned for us—**a life to the full** (John 10:10)—must be built on a strong and biblical spiritual foundation.

Although God draws us to him in many different ways, as disciples of Christ many of us are extremely blessed to have come to an educated decision regarding our faith through a study series commonly used within our fellowship. In various congregations, there are series entitled *First Principles, Shining Like Stars,* and *Equipping,* among other titles. These topical Bible studies can develop the spiritual foundation that all Christians need. The experience of processing and applying the Scriptures and the relationships built while studying these fundamental teachings are invaluable. Our relationship with God, discipleship, and the biblical principles learned through the study series are the foundation for everything in our lives. Without this foundation, all else could be labeled a "chasing after the wind"—a mere waste of time (Ecclesiastes 1:14).

Typically, during these studies, we make many educated decisions. The Bible studies call us to seek God and love him with all our heart, soul, strength, and mind (Luke 10:27). Topical studies may also include in-depth discussions on Jesus and grace. We study about the Bible being the authoritative word of God and make the decision to have God's word as the standard for our lives. Without that decision, we would not have had a chance to become Christians. We learn the Bible's definition of a disciple, or Christian. This is so important because if we take a poll of ten people, we just may end up with ten different definitions of what it means to be a Christian. I am extremely grateful for the disciples who sacrificed time, energy, gas, and more to share about God's kingdom along with his exciting purpose and mission for all his children.

Though we all know that rape and adultery are wrong, many of us are not as aware of the lists of sins in the Bible such as those in Mark 7, Galatians 5, and 2 Timothy 3. It is encouraging when disciples share their stories—the good, the bad, and the ugly—about the sins they have committed and how they repented of them. Personalizing the ways we have hurt God with our own sins (of commission and omission) can lead to the convictions needed in order to repent and become Christians. The realization that our sins actually separate us from God (Isaiah 59:1–2) can wake us up to alarming spiritual realities.

REFLECTION

1. Are you continually studying the Bible to apply it to your life? Do you understand what God's purpose and mission are for your life, as well as the Bible verses that delineate both?

   _____

   _____

   _____

During my freshman year of college, I was very grateful to study the cross of Christ, which led to a deeper understanding of the depth of God's love and Jesus' personal sacrifice. I remain committed to God today because of this foundational study of the crucifixion. I remember reading the medical account of what Jesus suffered physically for me. How powerful! Though Mel Gibson received tons of criticism about his movie, *The Passion of the Christ* was the closest many of us have ever seen to what Jesus actually suffered as a result of our sins and for our forgiveness. God's sacrificial love is still unfathomable (Matthew 26–27)! Amen that we can daily make the decision to die to sins and live for righteousness (1 Peter 2:21–25). God is so gracious!

I had always heard that repentance is confession. It was great to learn the actual definition of the word and the biblical meaning of repentance (Acts 2:38; Matthew 3:8, 4:17; Mark 1:15; Luke 3:8; Luke 13:1–5). Before studying the Bible, I desperately wanted to change and live for God but didn't know how. Nor did I have the power of God's Spirit to help me. Some of us had "accepted Jesus as our Savior" as many times as the doors of the church were opened, but never really had a significant change in our behavior or our understanding of God's attitude toward sin. Some of the best news I ever heard came as I learned of God's plan for the forgiveness of my sins through baptism (Acts 2:38; Acts 8; 1 Peter 3:21; Romans 6:3–4; Colossians 2:12; Matthew 28:19; Acts 22:16). The idea that all my sins (I wrote a list of them) could be totally wiped out was absolutely unbelievable. God's grace is utterly amazing!

REFLECTION

2. Have you ever studied out the sins that separate you from God, your sins that Jesus died for? If so, how long ago? Have you ever looked up the definition of repentance and studied it in the Bible? Have you ever read a medical account of the crucifixion? How did it impact you?

_____

_____

_____

_____

_____

_____

_____

_____

Our Bible studies would not be complete, and we could not make an educated decision, without looking at the varied teachings on how to become a Christian. If we took a poll on what the Bible says about how to become a Christian, we would get many different answers. But we know that God's word doesn't change and that we are not to preach a "different gospel" (Galatians 1:6–9).

Unfortunately, some of us have seen, heard, or been a part of horror stories in churches. It can sometimes be hard to see God amidst all the sin, church fights, church splits, and human confusion. Many of us grew up in dysfunctional and sinful families and churches. It might have been hard to even admit that our sins had damaged God's perfect plan for his church. The topical study of God's plan for the church (made up of us imperfect people) is encouraging and inspiring. Despite our own sinfulness, God planned for us to become a part of his family, the church. What a blessing and honor. In the study, we learn that Jesus is the head of the body and that we are members of the body (Colossians 1:18;

1 Corinthians 12). Disciples are aware that there is much to learn and yet are excited about how we can give to one another and help each other make it to heaven (Hebrews 3:12–13, 10:24–25). What an example the early church is for us to follow (Acts 2)!

Then, finally, as we decide to commit our lives and our all to Jesus, we "count the cost." Many of us read what Paul wrote in 1 Corinthians 15:1–2:

> Now, brothers and sisters, I want to remind you of the gospel I preached to you, which you received and on which you have taken your stand. By this gospel you are saved, if you hold firmly to the word I preached to you. Otherwise, you have believed in vain.

As we "counted the cost," we were also called to consider whether we would be committed to God for the rest of our lives. Then, knowing that God provides all we need and that grace saves us and will carry us until we die or Christ comes back— we took the plunge! We were baptized for the forgiveness of our sins. For those of you who have been through this Bible study and life-changing journey: Remember the feeling? Remember the joy? Remember the clarity? Remember the gratitude? Remember the commitment to be willing to go anywhere, do anything, and give up everything since God has done that for us? When was the last time you told your story to someone? God's power is seen through the amazing changes he made and continues to make in each of our lives. Let's encourage each other with our conversion stories and our continued efforts to become all the more like Christ.

If you are reading this book and have not yet had the opportunity to work through the study series I just described, I encourage you to find a fellowship close to you (on the www.disciplestoday. org Church Locator page), make the call, and begin the greatest journey ever!

REFLECTION

3. Do you attend a church fellowship where people have made educated decisions to have the Bible as the standard for their lives and to live as disciples in a love relationship with God? Is the church you attend a reflection of the New Testament church? Does your fellowship reflect the diversity of your country's population?

My Christian Story

I grew up attending Baptist churches in Northeast Washington, DC, Philadelphia, Pennsylvania, and Greensboro and McLeansville, North Carolina. When I turned sixteen and was able to work at a McDonalds in a Greensboro mall, I rarely attended services. Due to my family circumstances, I was determined to have money of my own. Though I was and am eternally and extremely grateful for the foundation of faith that was provided as I heard the amazing stories of God, Jesus, Abraham, Isaac, and Jacob, I found very little practical teaching or spiritual relationships that could help me to deal with peer pressure, decision-making, my parents separating and divorcing, an alcoholic stepfather, and other issues. I believed in God, wanted to do what was right, tried to be a "good person," and felt that because of these values and convictions, I would definitely make it to heaven. At the same time, I did not know how to deal with the many internal conflicts and the sadness that we often experience in our development.

Many times, I attempted to read the Bible, but I seldom studied it. Though I was considered intelligent, I had problems understanding the Elizabethan English used in the King James Version. For instance, in Job 30:27 the KJV says, "My bowels boiled, and rested not: the days of affliction prevented me." I so appreciate the folks who introduced me to the New International Version and additional, more current translations of the Bible. I can understand "The churning inside me never stops; days of suffering confront me."

God had a plan to meet my needs and help me know him, his love, and his purpose for my life. Though I had always planned to return to Philadelphia to attend Temple University, God had another plan. A volleyball coach from the University of North Carolina at Charlotte saw me play during a high school game. I had never thought about playing in college, but accepted the opportunity and changed plans. We had "boot camp" before school started...no one could call it practice. It was more like torture. Hardly any of us could walk after the first day. Unfortunately, I suffered a knee injury, had surgery to reattach my cartilage, and spent three months in a cast from my hip to my ankle. Though I was highly disappointed, my father expressed gratitude for the doctor and the cast. He didn't want me to return to playing and have my knee lock up while jumping to spike the ball.

I met many people as a result of the cast and crutches. One morning, as I waited for campus police transportation, Betty Herbert asked me if I needed assistance. I didn't, but we talked for a bit, and she invited me to visit her church. I was shocked, to say the least, because Betty is Caucasian. I surely was not aware of any interracial churches in North Carolina during the mid-1980s. I later visited and could only sit on the floor (in a red skirt), since the folding chairs would not accommodate an angled cast. I was blown away by the love expressed in the relationships I saw. More impactful yet were the members' desire and ability to answer my questions with scriptures. I was used to hearing all kinds of varying opinions, but I was not accustomed to seeing people who lived with the Bible as the standard for every aspect of their lives rather than traditions, emotions, leaders, or anything else.

I began to study the Bible with new friends from the Charlotte, North Carolina fellowship. I was so excited about the things I was learning that I invited friends to come to my studies. I guess I didn't remember or wasn't told that the studies were for me personally! To this day, I am grateful for Martha (Ann) and Debbie, who took the time to share with me the truths of God's word and their lives. For me today, that is one of the greatest joys I have: sharing God's word with others. He has changed me and my life completely!

4. How do your relationships help you, on a practical level, to live in accordance with God's word? Can you back up your spiritual beliefs with specific scriptures? How often do you use God's word to teach, rebuke, correct, and train yourself and fellow believers (2 Timothy 3:16–17)?

_____

_____

_____

_____

_____

_____

_____

_____

Chapter Four

Our Unconscious Mind Is in Control

If there is one thing that has revolutionized my life in the past few years and one thing that I would like others to understand, it is that **our subconscious mind controls approximately 95 percent** of what is happening in our personal worlds. Did you know that?

Before being introduced to Neuro-Linguistic Programming (NLP) and Time Line Therapy® in 2018, I hadn't given my unconscious mind much thought. I hadn't considered that I had both a conscious and subconscious mind. I just hadn't given this fact any attention. Of course, I had heard about the subconscious mind, but I had never considered its impact on me, my relationship with myself (including my self-concept), my relationship with God, my relationships with others, my behavior, my mental state, and even my physiology. Scientists estimate that 95 percent of our brain activity is unconscious and that our emotions, behavior, the decisions we make, and all the actions we take are driven by this unconscious/subconscious brain activity.

If you've ever felt stuck with unwanted behaviors or attitudes ("I'm not enough," etc.) or stuck with unhelpful lingering emotions (anger, sadness/grief, fear/worry/anxiety, hurt, guilt/shame, etc.), it's highly likely that it is because those things haven't been transformed or rewired at the subconscious level. We can consciously focus on changing behaviors, attitudes, cognitions (thoughts/perceptions), emotions, and ways of relating to others, but that "consciousness" reportedly addresses only 5 percent of what is happening in our lives! Since our unconscious mind is also considered "primal," it operates with a focus on emotion as opposed to logic or reason. Thus, **the emotions and memories that are stored in our subconscious mind must be rewired through our subconscious mind.** Just thinking about them, processing them, deciding to change them, or reframing them consciously will not root out the negative emotions and memories subconsciously.

I discuss many more details of this in *Spiritual Transformation: Emotional Intelligence and Freedom* (2020), but I do want to share the role of our unconscious mind here in order to reduce frustrations related to growth and change efforts. We humans have continually attempted to change solely with the use of our conscious minds. This can be considered akin to behavior management techniques and interventions; they do not typically get to the root of what is driving the unwanted behavior. As I mentioned in *Spiritual Transformation,* NLP trainers all over the world teach the following about the role (or prime directives, rules, commands) of the unconscious mind (Tad James, 2018):

1. **Stores memories**

2. Organizes all memories—makes associations; categorizes

3. **Represses memories** with unresolved negative emotional charges—sometimes called **emotional baggage,** where we can currently or in the future relive our past

4. Presents repressed memories for resolution—to make rational decisions and to release emotion

5. Runs the body—automatically runs basic physical functions based on blueprints

6. May keep the **repressed emotions** repressed for protection

7. Preserves the body

8. **Is the domain of the emotions—the part of us that feels**

9. Is a highly moral being—accepting the morality we've been taught and have accepted

10. Enjoys serving, needs clear orders to follow—needs to be consistent

11. **Controls and maintains all perceptions**—the ability to perceive can be increased

12. Generates, stores, distributes, and transmits **energy**—energy can be increased

13. Maintains instincts and generates habits

14. Needs repetition until a habit is installed

15. Is programmed to continually seek more and more—there is always more to discover

16. Functions best as a whole, integrated unit—incongruences need to be integrated

17. Is symbolic—uses and responds to symbols

18. Takes everything personally—the basis of "perception is projection"

19. Works on the principle of least effort—path of least resistance

20. Does not process negatives—omits the "not" in "do not fall;" needs positively worded statements (e.g., "watch your step")

That is a lot of information to digest. Yet it is imperative that we understand the role of the unconscious mind so that we can better access its power and optimize its working toward godly outcomes and the life to the full that God has planned for each of us. As I note and expound upon in *Spiritual Transformation,* the extent that our conscious and unconscious processes and mechanisms lie outside our awareness is the extent to which they control unconscious processes. In addition, optimal learning and change are considered to happen unconsciously or in tandem with the unconscious mind. **Frequently, good intentions are not enough for achieving our desired outcomes and goals.** Yet God always comes through with good news! In Hebrews 9:14, he tells us, "How much more, then, will the blood of Christ, who through the eternal Spirit offered himself unblemished to God, cleanse our consciences from acts that lead to death, so that we may serve the living God!" We can retrain our emotional circuitry for our own good and God's glory! Additional details on how we use our unconscious mind to rewire our neural circuitry is in Chapter 10 of *Spiritual Transformation* or on my website at www.cresenda-jones.com/coaching.

So if you have internalized our world and Christian culture's "matrimaniacal messages" (DePaulo, 2022) that can be spiritually and emotionally harmful, the good news is that those messages can be rewired. I emotionally and cognitively internalized the harmful perceptions that being married is better, more "spiritual," more desirable; and that I am not desirable, etc. Amen that we don't have to stay stuck in the negative emotions and limiting beliefs/decisions that can restrict or drown out God's plans for our lives. God's John 10:10 promise is not just for those who are married. God's plan for life to the full is for Paul, Jeremiah, Mary, Martha, and Jesus. God's plan through Jesus—"I came so they can have real and eternal life, more and better life than they ever dreamed of" (MSG)—is also for me and YOU.

REFLECTION

1. What roles/prime directives of our unconscious mind stand out to you the most? Why? How can this knowledge help you transform and mature spiritually and emotionally?

_____

_____

_____

_____

_____

_____

_____

_____

Chapter Five

Stuck in Limiting Beliefs

After my wedding cancellation and breakup, it took me a while to articulate the limiting beliefs/decisions that were stored in my subconscious mind. As I mentioned in the discussion on our subconscious minds, our emotions and memories are stored there. In relation to canceling our wedding and breaking up, I didn't understand why I was experiencing months and months of struggle, shock, grief, feeling lost, denial, depression, desperation for answers, bargaining, and anguish. It was nine months from the time we did not put the purchase offer on a home until God orchestrated a "breakthrough"—a change of mind for me. I did not want to be in the state I was in...but it took God's grace and mercy to provide a few ah-ha! moments when I understood that powerful **limiting beliefs/decisions were wreaking havoc** in my life, mind, and emotional state, and even in my physiology.

I want to state clearly that it is imperative that we process grief in healthy ways. It is imperative that we embrace, allow, and sit with our emotions (including grief), or we will be shackled by repressed or disallowed emotions later. It is important that we deal with emotional pain. And in the case of broken relationships, it is important that we grieve those "emotional amputations."

Yet I was at the point where I definitely felt that something was not going well in my grief journey regarding the ending of my relationship. Something seemed to be awry with the heartbreak I continued to feel. I felt completely stuck with the following thoughts/ beliefs:

- I am supposed to be married.
- It is NOT OK that I am single.
- I need to be married—I can't do this single thing any longer.
- I am supposed to be married to this man (that prayer for the Men of Freedom II group).
- I really need him.
- I am supposed to be married to my best friend.
- Together, we can have an amazing relationship.
- Together, we can and are supposed to have the Kingdom News Network (KNN) story (his dream).
- Together, we can manage the challenges in relationship dynamics and be great partners.
- Together, we can be used by God to make a great difference in our world.

In reality, it doesn't take multiple limiting beliefs to derail our life to the full that God has planned—just one such belief can do great damage. As you know, Satan has come to steal, kill, and destroy (John 10:10). Satan will use anything and everything to accomplish his task. A simple limiting belief (like "I should be married," or "I am not enough") can wreak havoc in our lives, gratitude, clarity, freedom, impact, character, personality, relationships, goals, and dreams.

I do want to note that some of those beliefs listed are true in some relationships. Yet these things were no longer true for my relationship. If I continued to stick with these beliefs, thoughts, or cognitions, I would only extend my pain and heartache. I chose (and still have to choose daily) not to do that.

In order to understand how we can easily be stuck with unhelpful and even harmful perceptions (internal representations), it's important to understand the **NLP Communication Model** (James, n.d.) and how our brain works. God made our brains in a way that we can handle the huge amount of information that comes at us. As the figure shows, we take in events using our senses—what we see, hear, feel, taste, smell, and even our own self-talk. Once we experience an event, we process

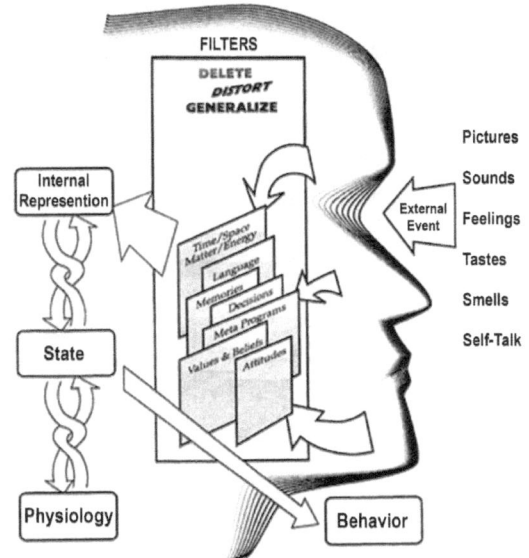

everything through the filters God has given us. In our minds, we all filter as we delete, distort, and generalize external events. We also have filters that include our language, past decisions, values, beliefs, and attitudes. The one filter that is least familiar and that everyone asks about is that of metaprograms. Metaprograms "are powerful mental processes that help people manage, guide, and direct their experiences. They help us decide what to pay attention to and we distort, delete, and generalize the rest. After all, the conscious mind can only pay attention to so many moving parts at any given time" (Robbins, n.d.). Once our minds have filtered the input, we have created an internal representation or perception of each event. This internal representation is how we view or perceive things in our lives.

It is critically important and helpful to understand that our internal representations are interdependent with our emotional state and our physiology. The most powerful thing about this model of interacting is that **our internal representations lead to our behavior.** Thus, as Dr. Daniel Amen notes, if we change our brain, we can indeed change our lives! If we want different behaviors that are more in line with God's life to the full, we need to change our subconscious internal representations.

Even if you are not stuck because of limiting beliefs that relate to a relationship, possibly you are stuck with some of the more general limiting beliefs/decisions I commonly see with my clients. These beliefs/decisions insidiously and subconsciously hinder or destroy us spiritually, mentally, emotionally, socially, and physically. These beliefs that are stored in our subconscious minds must be rewired there. Here are just a few of the highly common and harmful beliefs/decisions that can drive our behavior and self-sabotage us:

- I am not enough; I know I will fail.
- I have to be perfect; it's not OK to make mistakes—my humanity is not acceptable.
- I am responsible for (versus to) others; I have to fix situations and people.
- I cannot handle this person/these people; I am afraid I cannot handle this.
- I don't deserve to be a priority; my feelings and thoughts are not worthy of consideration.
- My needs are not important; I need to hide my emotions and thoughts.
- I don't have valuable contributions; I don't have anything to offer.
- I allow others to make decisions for me; I allow others to repeatedly hurt me.
- I need to fix everything.
- God can work in others' lives but not in mine; Time Line Therapy® will work for everyone but me.
- I fear that I will be abandoned; I have to agree with/please others so that they do not abandon me.
- It is unrighteous to challenge authority figures/leaders.
- I am not smart enough or spiritual enough to speak up; I have no voice.

- Self-value and self-care are selfish; I have to earn love and devotion; I don't deserve love; others are "better" than me and more important.

- I am all alone.

- I have to settle; I am asking for too much.

- I can't trust myself.

- I fear criticism.

- I will not be successful.

Circling back to the breakup of my relationship and the limiting beliefs and decisions that kept me stuck, I am very grateful that God continues to lead me through the stages of grief to acceptance (we are not meant to be together) and hope (I'm perfectly fine with God, with unknowns, with being single, and without my ex-fiancé). Please note that single folks are not the only ones with these limiting beliefs/decisions. My married clients are challenged by Satan in similar ways. God has given me more than I could ever ask or imagine, through his Spirit, in the focus on creating my life to the full right now...not just for me, but for others too. This relationship and experience led me to support others who have to manage challenges in their marital relationships, including a couple of my closest friends. If we align ourselves with God's will, he can take a "mess" and turn it into a "message" that will be a healing ministry with eternal impact!

REFLECTION

1. Can you relate to any of the limiting beliefs/decisions I listed regarding my past relationship?

   _____

   _____

---

2. Have you recognized that no matter how much you read your Bible and pray, some undesired beliefs and behaviors are just stuck with you (driven by your subconscious mind)?

---

3. What are the limiting beliefs/decisions that stand in the way of God's plan for you to live a life to the full (John 10:10)?

Chapter Six

At Cause Versus Being at Effect

Do not be deceived: God cannot be mocked. **A man reaps what he sows.** *Whoever sows to please their flesh, from the flesh will reap destruction; whoever sows to please the Spirit, from the Spirit will reap eternal life. Let us not become weary in doing good, for* **at the proper time we will reap a harvest if we do not give up.** *(Galatians 6:7–9, emphasis added)*

Shallow men believe in luck. Strong men believe in cause and effect.　　　　　—Ralph Waldo Emerson

Goodness, have I had some challenging conversations with people who spoke, communicated, and lived as victims, but who would want to attack me when I pointed it out...as opposed to dealing with the issues at hand! In the Time Line Therapy® breakthrough process I facilitate with clients, we have to check to see if someone is "at cause" or "at effect." There are a couple of really tough questions in the Detailed Personal History (of the Time Line Therapy® breakthrough process), where we figure out someone's "root issue" or "greater problem." The greater problem is what causes all the problems they

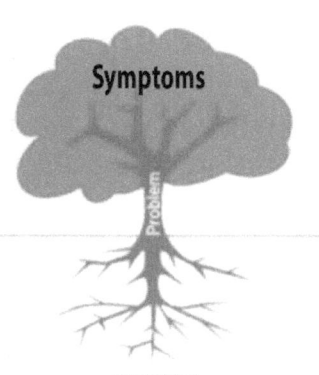

would like to alleviate. Because the questions can be a bit offensive, I preface them by saying that I did not develop the questions and that they are highly effective in uncovering beliefs and emotions that are keeping the client stuck. The following are the most common root causes of my clients to date (both marrieds and singles), or what we call the "greater problem":

- Low self-esteem/confidence/value/worth, inferiority, worthlessness; feeling not good enough
- Fear/worry/anxiety
- Self-hatred
- Depression (sadness/grief)
- Repressed/unresolved emotions
- Codependency
- Perfectionism
- Shame (about own humanity)
- Unprocessed grief and hurts
- Not managing emotions well—anger, hurt, etc.
- Trauma and adverse childhood experiences (ACEs)

After we figure out a client's root cause or greater problem, just imagine me asking, "When did you choose to have these symptoms?"; "Why did your unconscious mind choose to create this?"; and "What do you gain as a result of this greater problem?" I make sure I remind my clients that I did not develop the questions, but that they are a part of the thirteen questions we need to ask in order to eliminate their root issue (greater problem). When I did my own personal Time Line Therapy® breakthrough process and worked on eliminating the negative emotions and limiting beliefs/decisions connected to past events, I had to consider this: How could I have possibly caused my greater problem of not accepting my humanity? I believe that I created the "never enough" modus operandi in order to be able to work to "be enough" in the minds of significant adults in my life. Unfortunately, I had internalized the "never enough" limiting belief and it was held in my unconscious mind.

REFLECTION

1. As you consider how things are going in your life (spiritually, emotionally/mentally, in your relationships, professionally, biologically/physically, and financially), if you could wake up tomorrow and everything be EXACTLY as you desire, what would you want to be different? How would your life look and feel? Make a list.

_____

_____

_____

_____

_____

_____

_____

_____

2. Now, what would you say could possibly be your "greater problem," the thing that causes all your presenting problems? What is fueling the challenges in your life… the things you want to be different? If you did know—what is your "greater problem"?

_____

_____

_____

_____

_____

_____

_____

_____

3. Regarding your greater problem, when and why do you think it was created? What secondary benefits/gains are connected to your greater problem?

_____

_____

_____

_____

_____

_____

_____

Most of us took science classes when we were in school and studied at least a bit of physical science. Causality is the study of how things influence one another, how causes lead to effects. You may recall that the effect, outcome, result, or event happens because of a cause. Sometimes, when we are attempting to be intentional, we ask ourselves what will happen when we make certain choices. In some cases, cause and effect are straightforward. In other cases, cause-and-effect relationships may be more complex and less apparent. When we can articulate what happens and why it happens, we can explain a relationship. We have a cause-and-effect universe and **we (consciously or unconsciously) cause things to happen in our personal lives.** Considering cause and effect is not about placing blame or finding fault. Accepting responsibility allows us to take control of what God has allowed us to have control over—ourselves. Instead of spending our energy on blame and fault, we can use our emotional energy on thoughts and plans for much better things. We can focus that energy on the actions we need to take toward our desired outcomes and effects. We can invest that energy in what we do control.

In NLP and the Time Line Therapy® breakthrough process training, I learned that **life does not happen to us, but that it happens through us.** We are at cause, meaning that on many levels we are the cause of what is happening in our lives. For everything we do, for every action we take, there is a reaction. That is basic physical science. In order to live lives to the full (John 10:10), we have to accept that in many ways we are the creator. We create our experiences, and if we want different results, we must take responsibility for our current results and cause different ones. **We create our experiences on many levels.** You may have heard of locus of control. Locus of control is "the degree to which people believe that they personally, as opposed to external forces (beyond their influence), have control over the outcome of events in their lives" (Wikipedia, n.d.). Julian B. Rotter helped us to understand that we have, along a continuum, varying degrees of an internal or external locus of control. With an internal **locus of control,** we believe that we control our own lives. With an external locus of control, we believe that people and circumstances beyond us control our lives. A person who has that external locus of control is someone who lives at effect or with a victim mindset.

On one hand, being at cause is highly encouraging in the sense that we can do our part to create: to decide to have and cause the life that God has planned and that we desire. On the other hand, as Eleanor Roosevelt noted, "Freedom makes a huge requirement of every human being. With freedom comes responsibility. For the person who is unwilling to grow up, the person who does not want to carry his own weight, this is a frightening prospect." We can either live as victims or live at cause.

REFLECTION

4. Are you a person who typically lives with an internal or external locus of control? How is this evident in your life?

_____

Many are not "at cause" because of **secondary gains.** Secondary gain is when the benefits of having a problem outweigh getting rid of the problem. With each of the greater problems in the list above, there can be secondary gains. From clients, I mainly have heard of the temptations of not wanting to be held responsible, not wanting to risk conflict or failure, or not wanting others to have expectations in line with one's gifts and abilities. With codependency, secondary gains frequently include the choice to deal with everyone else's problems and ignore the pain of our own. With perfectionism, a secondary gain can be not having to deal with the disappointment of others. Satan will do all he can to steal, kill, and destroy (John 10:10). We have to decide that we want to please God and enjoy life to the full more than we want to live with and in our problems.

For me, being at cause brings to mind the scripture in Hebrews 4:13, where it says, "Nothing in all creation is hidden from God's sight. Everything is uncovered and laid bare before the eyes of him to whom we must give account." On one hand, it is comforting to know that God sees everything, since we often experience injustices because of someone else's sin or oversight. Many times, I have felt that I may as well "make [my] calling and election sure" (2 Peter 1:10 KJ21) by being vulnerable, open, and asking for help, since God already knows everything. I may as well be completely honest and open since God already knows and has provided everything I need for life and godliness (2 Peter 1:3 KJ21). I just have to choose what he has provided. On the other hand, if we do not want to change, Hebrews 4 can feel very weighty—understanding that God knows everything about us and recognizing that we will give an account.

It's been said that insanity is doing the same thing over and over and expecting different results. As my friend James Campbell includes in his email signature, "We can't solve problems by using the same kind of thinking we used when we created them." The bottom line is that we have a choice. We can accept that our actions—what we do over and over—cause results. Or we can attempt to "wash our hands" (like Pilate in Matthew 27:24) and be victims to what is happening around us and what we allow to happen to us. We each are responsible for getting the results that God and we desire. We each are responsible for doing our part in realizing our desired outcomes.

The great news is that when we ask, God will provide. When we seek, we will find. And, when we take action—when we knock—the door will be opened (Matthew 7:7). Jesus came so that we can have life and have it to the full (John 10:10). He is our Good Shepherd—we just need to ensure that we're doing all we can to be in the right pen! We need to take responsibility, as far as it depends on us (Romans 12:18), for our choices, efforts, focus, priorities, values, limitations, strengths, and intentions, and the resulting outcomes. We especially can control what is going on inside us—in our minds and with our emotions, behavior, and reactions. We can even be in control of what we believe to be true.

When we are at cause, as far as it is up to us, we can change, and we can get the results we desire. It's so awesome that we have God's Holy Spirit power—the same Spirit that raised Jesus from the dead (Romans 8:11). When God's Spirit is living in us, nothing is impossible (Luke 1:37)! Let's not be victims. Let's not waste our precious time here on earth focused on who is to blame, but let's ensure that we do what we can with what we do control. Let's decide to constantly tap into God's power and our own agency so that God will be glorified and so that we can live life to the full! I LOVE the serenity prayer and, with my Time Line Therapy® process, it was one of the learnings that allowed me to easily and effortlessly eliminate negative emotions and limiting beliefs connected to past events. I have included it here, the way I state it, with my substitutions italicized. This rendering allows my unconscious mind to accept the prayer (remember, our unconscious mind does not record negatives – Chapter 4):

God grant me the serenity
to accept the things others control (for "I cannot change");
courage to change the things I can;
and wisdom to know the difference.

Living one day at a time;
enjoying one moment at a time;
accepting hardships as the pathway to peace;
taking, as he did, this sinful world
as it is, *as opposed to how I would have it* (for "not as I would have it");
trusting that he will make all things right
if I surrender to his will;
that I may be reasonably happy in this life
and supremely happy with him
forever in the next.
Amen.

REFLECTION

5. Would you say that you live a life that is aligned with the serenity prayer? A life of serenity, acceptance, courage, trust, surrender, and joy as you keep your mind set on things above (Colossians 3:2)?

_____

_____

_____

_____

_____

_____

_____

_____

6. What scriptures come to mind that support a life of serenity?

    _____

    _____

    _____

    _____

    _____

    _____

Living at cause can feel risky. I recall counting the cost of opening a private school for the underserved in Philadelphia, Pennsylvania. Though my father was a very cautious man, I will never forget the conversation we had as I sought his input on whether to move forward and use the church building we were offered for our endeavor. Despite being a highly logical, guarded, prudent, and vigilant man, my dad was all for me stepping out of my comfort zone to try to meet the needs of children who many consider "throwaways." I was shocked by his response. The main thing that stood out to me was his encouragement to NOT have any regrets. He did not want me to cower regarding the unknowns and risks and then later regret not taking the chance to make a difference in others' lives. In the *Healing for Damaged Emotions Workbook,* David Seamands talks about "shouldas, couldas, and wouldas." God doesn't want us to live in those prisons. I hope and pray that we all can make it to heaven with as few regrets as possible! *Carpe diem.*

REFLECTION

7. What will you regret NOT doing if you don't do it before your life comes to an end? What have you allowed to stand in your way? How can you responsibly be at cause?

    _____

_____

_____

_____

_____

_____

_____

Please continue to get all the help you need (Proverbs 20:18). **Seek competent input!** Seek out those who have awareness, knowledge, skills, and experience (Proverbs 12:22). Continue to ask, seek, and knock. Continue to consider whether you have given your power away or you are walking in step with God and his Spirit. Consider what you are attracting in your life. Consider whether you are taking responsibility for your own life and outcomes. Even when undesirable events happen, we still can take responsibility for learning from those events. When we do not take responsibility, we set ourselves up as powerless victims. We can ask ourselves what learnings are needed...what wisdom we can take away from each and every event. Though I started working with a professional counselor in 2000, it was not until 2018 that I learned about my subconscious mind and the Time Line Therapy® breakthrough process. I could waste emotional energy wishing that I had these resources before 2018, but I choose not to do that. God provides everything we need for life and godliness—at the perfect times (Romans 8:28). Let's "play full out"—giving 100 percent so that we can experience life to the full (John 10:10). Let's press on to take hold of that for which Christ Jesus took hold of us and made us his own (Philippians 3:12)!

Below you will find additional scriptures to reflect on that contain principles related to cause and effect. Please consider how your life is in line with each of these scriptures. Celebrate God's power and grace working through you. You may also need to consider what type of decisions need to be made in order to more fully live out God's purpose in your life.

Colossians 3:23–24

Whatever you do, work heartily, as for the Lord and not for men, knowing that from the Lord you will receive the inheritance as your reward (ESV).

Matthew 7:24–27

"Therefore everyone who hears these words of mine and puts them into practice is like a wise man who built his house on the rock. The rain came down, the streams rose, and the winds blew and beat against that house; yet it did not fall, because it had its foundation on the rock. But everyone who hears these words of mine and does not put them into practice is like a foolish man who built his house on sand. The rain came down, the streams rose, and the winds blew and beat against that house, and it fell with a great crash."

Hosea 10:12

Sow righteousness for yourselves,
*   reap the fruit of unfailing love,*
and break up your unplowed ground;
*   for it is time to seek the Lord,*
until he comes
*   and showers his righteousness on you.*

Matthew 8:8

The centurion replied, "Lord, I do not deserve to have you come under my roof. But just say the word, and my servant will be healed."

Matthew 9:37

Then he said to his disciples, "The harvest is plentiful but the workers are few."

John 5:5–6

One who was there had been an invalid for thirty-eight years. When Jesus saw him lying there and learned that he had been in this condition for a long time, he asked him, "Do you want to get well?"

Isaiah 50:10–11 (MSG)

Who out there fears God,
> *actually listens to the voice of his servant?*

For anyone out there who doesn't know where you're going,
> *anyone groping in the dark,*

Here's what: Trust in God.
> *Lean on your God!*

But if all you're after is making trouble,
> *playing with fire,*

Go ahead and see where it gets you.
> *Set your fires, stir people up, blow on the flames,*

But don't expect me to just stand there and watch.
> *I'll hold your feet to those flames.*

REFLECTION

8. Regarding the scriptures above, what new, renewed, or deepened convictions do you have? What decisions have you made?

_____

_____

_____

_____

_____

_____

_____

_____

_____

_____

_____

Chapter Seven

My New Decisions and Keys to Achievable Outcomes

Being single once again, I did not enjoy my time of grief, great emotional distress, anguish, numbness, heartbreak, denial, depression, longing, and bargaining (typical stages of grief). The struggle with my thoughts and emotions regarding the ending of my relationship was highly challenging. I wanted to be able to "move on" and "move forward." I wanted to accept my ex-fiancé's choices. I wanted to focus on what God wanted me to be and do after our decision to end the relationship. I just could not get there.

With Time Line Therapy®, new cognitions (beliefs and decisions) are established in our subconscious minds. This is very important to understand. I had already consciously thought, understood, decided, and desired to embody new decisions, but, since there were other tapes playing in my subconscious mind (Chapter 4), I was fighting a losing battle against them. One of my favorite Bruce Lipton quotes says that our thoughts are mainly controlled by our subconscious, and **you cannot change the subconscious mind by just thinking about it.** "The subconscious mind is like a tape player. Until you change the tape, it will not change." I am very grateful for the efficiency and effectiveness of Time Line Therapy® techniques in providing the subconscious rewiring I so desperately needed. I was stuck with my stinking thinking and limiting beliefs. The emotions connected to grief and my internal representations felt debilitating.

After God allowed me to figure out that I needed new subconscious learnings or cognitions (it took me long enough!), I went to work. I realized that the limiting beliefs that were stuck in my subconscious mind needed to be rewired. Over a couple of days (approximately forty minutes total), I replaced those limiting beliefs/decisions with the following new ones:

- God is with me (I am not alone), God's got me, God loves me.
- I have had a very full life and I decide to have life to the full now.
- I am and will be content no matter the circumstances... no matter my status.
- I have wonderful relationships and highly meaningful activities in my life.
- I deserve and am made for mutually beneficial connections.
- I am grateful for my life.
- I am strong, lovable, valuable, and worthy of protection, sacrifice, and being a priority.
- I am blessed and highly favored.
- I am God's beloved daughter.
- I trust God to meet my needs.
- I am "to die for."
- I love and protect myself.
- I choose healthy relationships.
- I choose serenity (prayer).
- I choose to allow my rational brain to override the romanticizing of unhealthy relationships and infatuations.
- I choose to face the truth of others' decisions.
- I accept others' decisions regarding their emotional and mental health.
- Others are responsible for their own spiritual, emotional, mental, and social health.

The Impact

After using Time Line Therapy® techniques, which rewire subconscious neural pathways, I was blown away that I then felt that I could breathe. I hadn't realized that it seemed like I was holding my breath from the time that I decided that the relationship, as it was, would not be healthy. I may have been "holding my breath" even longer. With all that had been going on in my life (my mom's dementia, being her caretaker, wedding cancellation, and the ending of my relationship), I had noticed an emotional and physical heaviness. I mentioned to a friend that it seemed like I had aged considerably in my countenance. It is amazing, as the NLP Communication Model notes (Chapter 5), that our physiology is interdependent with our emotional state and our internal representations (subconscious and conscious perceptions). After gaining the wisdom (learnings) from the Time Line Therapy® elimination of my limiting beliefs/decisions, I felt like a weight had been lifted off my body, mind, soul, and spirit. It reminded me of when I was first introduced to Time Line Therapy® by the supervisor for my master's degree in professional counseling. After I volunteered for a demonstration, the limiting belief of "I am not enough" was eliminated. Classmates noted that it seemed like I'd had a face lift. Once again, God provided relief from the heaviness that limiting beliefs and negative emotions inflict!

REFLECTION

1. What events in your life have left you feeling aged and weighed down in your mind, body, soul, and spirit?

    _____

    _____

    _____

    _____

    _____

_____

_____

_____

2. Though you've consciously done all you can to think
   and believe differently and to think in accordance with
   God's word, what negative emotions (anger, sadness/
   grief, fear/worry/anxiety, hurt, guilt/shame), limiting
   beliefs, stinking thinking, or tapes still impact you or
   dog you out?

_____

_____

_____

_____

_____

_____

Despite being single yet again, I am very grateful (consciously
and subconsciously) that God provides what we need so that we
can bask in his love, continue our journeys of loving him with all
our heart, soul, strength, and mind, and continue to work to love
others as ourselves (Luke 10:27). No matter our status, we can live
life to the full (John 10:10)!

Now that I have used Time Line Therapy® to clean out my
brain (swept the house clean – Matthew 12:43–45), I have rewired
those subconscious tapes that control approximately 95 percent
of our lives. As I noted in *Spiritual Transformation,* our emotional
state and physiology are so completely connected that a positive
mood brings to our remembrance positive memories, and a negative mood (anger, fear, hurt, guilt, anxiety, worry, sadness, etc.)
causes us to recall more challenging memories. Researchers have
found that mild mood changes affect our thinking. This is all the
more reason that God implores us to think about whatever is true,
noble, right, pure, lovely, admirable, excellent, or praiseworthy

(Philippians 4:8 – see Chapter 11). Imagine what a daily habit of such godly thinking could produce! We can choose which neural circuits we repeatedly wire together as we consciously recall that they fire together. Let's keep the Philippians 4 thoughts firing!

3. In general, which kind of thoughts, moods, and memories have you allowed to become hardwired in your brain (positive or negative)? What type of thoughts would you like to work toward repeatedly wiring together?

_____

_____

_____

_____

_____

_____

Keys to an Achievable Outcome

One additional NLP tool that came to mind as I was grieving the loss of my best friend and fiancé was the NLP "Keys to an Achievable Outcome" questions. Early on after my practitioner and master practitioner level trainings, I added scriptures to the questions and shared this tool with others. I'll share here what I thought as I worked toward getting my mind and emotional state to one of contentment, acceptance, being present, and peace. I will also include the worksheet tool for your personal use (Appendix 1) and have it posted on my website (www.cresendajones.com).

The scriptures (with emphasis added) that I connected with all the "Keys to an Achievable Outcome" questions were:

> And the LORD answered me: **"Write the vision;** *make it plain on tablets, so that it can be read on the run. For still the vision awaits its appointed time; it points to the end; aches for the coming—it will not lie. If it seems slow, wait*

for it; it will surely come; it will come right on time." **(Habakkuk 2:2–3 ESV and MSG combined)**

*Now to him who is able to do **far more abundantly beyond** all that we ask or think, according to the power that works within us, to him be the glory in the church and in Christ Jesus to all generations forever and ever. Amen.* **(Ephesians 3:20–21 NASB)**

*Forgetting what lies behind and straining forward to what lies ahead, **I press on toward the goal** for the prize of the upward call of God in Christ Jesus.* **(Philippians 3:13–14 ESV)**

Below are my thoughts (a personal sample) as I struggled through processing the questions and trying to figure out, in my grief, what exactly needed to be my desired and achievable outcomes. We put the brakes on our relationship in early July 2021, and I consciously thought through this NLP tool and began recording my thoughts in April 2022.

KEYS TO AN ACHIEVABLE OUTCOME

Desired outcome: Focused on relationships and activities that bring me joy and not stuck holding onto a relationship with ex-fiancé.

How is it possible that I don't have it now?
1. Grieving the end of the relationship
2. Goals and plans regarding future marriage relationship were in subconscious mind and on timeline...they need to be replaced
3. Grief with Mom's deterioration and dementia caregiving responsibilities
4. Personal/chronic health challenges

1. Stated in the positive.

What specifically do I want? Joy, contentment, release of ex-fiancé, rational brain kicking in (vs. emotional romanticizing), to be focused on relationships and activities that bring me joy, living in the present (vs. the past)

> **Philippians 4:8–9** – *Finally, brothers and sisters, whatever is true, whatever is noble, whatever is right, whatever is pure, whatever is lovely, whatever is admirable—if anything is excellent or praiseworthy—think about such things. Whatever you have learned or received or heard from me, or seen in me—put it into practice. And the God of peace will be with you.*

2. Specify present situation.

Where am I now? Inexpressible and overwhelming grief regarding end of the relationship, Mom's continued decline and care needs, personal health challenges. (Stages of grief: shock and denial; pain and guilt; anger and bargaining; depression, loneliness, and reflection; upward turn; reconstruction; acceptance and hope)

> **Romans 12:3** – *For by the grace given me I say to every one of you: Do not think of yourself more highly than you ought, but rather think of yourself with sober judgment, in accordance with the faith God has distributed to each of you.*

3. Specify outcome.

What will I see, hear, feel, etc., when I have it?

As if now. Make compelling. Insert in future (Time Line Therapy® Creating Your Future technique).

- Staying in the present
- Deciding not to ruminate on and romanticize the relationship—thinking only of what I miss as opposed to a balanced recollection
- Accept the reality of what is as opposed to what could be..."if only" stinking thinking

- Allowing myself to grieve—to feel the anguish regarding broken commitments/promises and mistakes

- Recalling who I am to God—his beloved daughter

- Recalling how God sees me and feels about me—I am "to die for"

- Gratitude for all the blessings I have—focusing on what I want (my achievable/desired outcomes) and watching my evaluations—the messages to my unconscious mind

- Consistent connecting with friends/loved ones—especially when I feel I want to talk to my ex-fiancé

- Holding onto learnings/wisdom from Time Line Therapy® techniques; clearing vs. rehearsing limiting beliefs and stinking thinking

- Focused on God's purpose for me at this time—continuing to invest in relationships with God and friends; learning more about Mom's dementia; writing book #3; facilitating book #2 discussion groups; serving clients; preparing for World Discipleship Summit class; optimizing personal physical health (exercising when possible and meal planning)

Mark 11:22–24 – *"Have faith in God," Jesus answered. "Truly I tell you, if anyone says to this mountain, 'Go, throw yourself into the sea,' and does not doubt in their heart but believes that what they say will happen, it will be done for them. Therefore I tell you, whatever you ask for in prayer, believe that you have received it, and it will be yours."*

Proverbs 18:21 – *The tongue has the power of life and death, and those who love it will eat its fruit.*

Matthew 21:22 – *"If you believe, you will receive whatever you ask for in prayer."*

2 Corinthians 4:13 – *It is written: "I believed; therefore I have spoken." Since we have that same spirit of faith, we also believe and therefore speak.*

Hebrews 11 – *Faith in action*
Proverbs 29:18 – *Where there is no revelation, people cast off restraint; but blessed is the one who heeds wisdom's instruction.*
Proverbs 29:18 KJ21 – *Where there is no vision, the people perish; but he that keepeth the law, happy is he.*
Isaiah 43:19 – *See, I am doing a new thing! Now it springs up; do you not perceive it? I am making a way in the wilderness and streams in the wasteland.*

4. Specify evidence procedure.

How will I know when I have it? Focused on relationships and activities that bring me joy; not stuck holding onto relationship

- No longer yearning for contact with ex-fiancé—heart, emotional, and mindset shifts

- No longer stuck in unhelpful, unwarranted, and inappropriate sadness/grief/bargaining

- Focused on who I am now (single again), what I am doing, and God's current plan for my life—living in the present and accepting current status

- Feeling content about my status

- Knowing I am OK single

- Seeking out support (that my ex-fiancé previously provided) from others

- Enjoying intimate fellowship with friends

- Working to make an eternal difference in others' lives (disciples and non-disciples)

  Proverbs 21:5 – *The plans of the diligent lead to profit as surely as haste leads to poverty.*

5. Is it congruently desirable? Yes.

What will this outcome get for me or allow me to do? Sooo much!

- Choosing to be content now

- Choosing to continue to be grateful now

- Choosing to continue to be happy now

- Choosing to continue to trust God and God's plan

- Choosing to continue to live life to the full now

- Choosing to continue to make a difference now

- Choosing to continue to honor and glorify God now!

- Praying consistently through ACTS—adoration, confession, thanksgiving, supplication

- Spiritual meditations

> **Jeremiah 29:11 AMPC** – *For I know the thoughts and plans that I have for you, says the Lord, thoughts and plans for welfare and peace and not for evil, to give you hope in your final outcome.*
>
> **Proverbs 3:6** – *In all your ways submit to him, and he will make your paths straight.*

6. Is it self-initiated and self-maintained? Both—with God's power

Is it only for me? Mainly, but for me and God and my loved ones

Colossians 3:2 – *Set your minds on things above, not on earthly things.*

7. Is it appropriately contextualized?

Where, when, how, and with whom do I want it?

- Everywhere—especially when so many things remind me of my ex-fiancé

- Now—finally

- Through Time Line Therapy® techniques (subconsciously eliminating negative emotions and limiting beliefs connected to past events), setting my mind and reliance on God and friends daily

- With God, me, and friends (especially close sisters and brothers in Christ)

  1 Corinthians 12:12–27 – *Unity and diversity in the body*

8. What resources are needed?
What do I have now and what do I need to get my outcome?

- God, God's Spirit, God's word, God's love, friends, friends' prayers, determination, perseverance, grit, resilience, purpose, mission, plans, peace, patience, kindness (to self), hope, faithfulness, self-control (EQ), Time Line Therapy® (to rewire limiting beliefs), wise input from friends, books (more than enough resources to process/learn from, think through and apply), competent classmates, all that I need for life and godliness, classmate to do Time Line Therapy® techniques with me, gospel music, and meditation

- Daily decisions to set my mind, review/listen to my learnings from Time Line Therapy®, mental space, and time (Mom to participate in adult daycare)

  Isaiah 40:31 – *Those who hope in the Lord will renew their strength. They will soar on wings like eagles; they will run and not grow weary, they will walk and not be faint.*

  Jeremiah 17:7 – *But blessed is the one who trusts in the Lord, whose confidence is in him.*

  Matthew 6:33 – *"But seek first his kingdom and his righteousness, and all these things will be given to you as well."*

  Matthew 19:26 – *Jesus looked at them and said, "With man this is impossible, but with God all things are possible."*

  Matthew 21:22 – *"If you believe, you will receive whatever you ask for in prayer."*

  Romans 8:28 – *And we know that in all things God works for the good of those who love him, who have been called according to his purpose.*

Have I ever had or done this before? Yes. With many disappointments or challenges. Was engaged before and did not get married. Many types of challenges in my life.

Do I know anyone who has? I'm sure…have to think through this…only one person comes to mind off the top of my head. That's comforting…that others have made decisions based on prayers that only what would glorify God in their lives will be done.

Can I act as if I have it? Yes…it's done!

9. Is it ecological?

For what purpose do I want this? Personal health—spiritual, emotional, mental, physical

What will I gain or lose if I have it? Gain—serenity, contentment, impact (current activities—book discussion groups and clients), focus, fun, completion of grief, etc. Lose—wasting time, wasting emotional energy, negative impact on health, allowing Satan to steal my power, etc.

What will happen if I get it? God better and more glorified, finishing book #3, contentment, being present, enjoying life, making plans, caring for Mom and being present with her, etc.

What won't happen if I get it? Won't waste time, let Satan win, won't miss opportunities to love and support others, won't feel sick physically, put off personal needs and projects

What will happen if I don't get it? Satan wins, choosing depression/grief, choosing to be paralyzed, missed opportunities

What won't happen if I don't get it? God being glorified, contentment, peace, serenity, living life to the full, making the most of every opportunity (Ephesians 5:16; Colossians 4:5), joy, gratitude, impact through supporting others, etc.

> **Isaiah 32:8** – *But the noble make noble plans, and by noble deeds they stand.*
>
> **John 4:34** – *"My food," said Jesus, "is to do the will of him who sent me and to finish his work."*
>
> **Romans 12:2** – *Do not conform to the pattern of this world, but be transformed by the renewing of your mind. Then you will be able to test and approve what God's will is—his good, pleasing and perfect will.*

> *So do not throw away your confidence; it will be richly re-*
> *warded. You need to persevere so that when you have done*
> *the will of God, you will receive what he has promised.* (He-
> brews 10:35–36)

Adapted from Tad James Co., LLC (2018). Time Line Therapy® Practitioner Training Manual

---

Processing "Keys to an Achievable Outcome" questions is immeasurably helpful. The time invested in focusing on our desired
outcomes and planning to achieve them is well worth it. I hope
that my personal example of working through these questions will
inspire and lead you to determine what you want in your life...and
to seize the day today! Since it was approximately nine months
before I thought about using this NLP tool, you get some idea of
the depth of the grief that I was processing. I am very grateful that
God provides tools like this and Time Line Therapy® so that we
can get the mental and emotional aspects of our being in line with
his will for our life and our spirituality.

REFLECTION

1. How was it helpful to read through my real-life sample
   of processing "Keys to an Achievable Outcome" questions?

   _____
   _____
   _____
   _____
   _____
   _____

_____

_____

2. Which desired outcome in your life can you process with
    these questions? Please access a blank copy of "Keys to
    an Achievable Outcome" in Appendix I or on my web-
    site (www.cresendajones.com) and work through the
    questions.

_____

_____

_____

_____

_____

_____

· Chapter Eight ·

What Good Is It? – Mark 8:36

*After all, what good is it for a man to gain the whole world
and yet forfeit his soul?* (Mark 8:36 EHV)

I feel incredibly blessed that God allowed me to be a math major twice (BA and M.Ed.). I also worked as a vice principal at a middle school and served as a principal of an elementary school. I then served as both a mathematics and science supervisor of curriculum, instruction, and assessment in school districts. Moreover, in my "full life," I worked to obtain both an MBA and an MA in professional counseling as part of my journey toward what I wanted to do vocationally, for my own personal growth, and in order to have greater competence in my efforts to support others. I then went for specialized training after my MA in professional counseling...once again, for personal growth and healing. But...**what good is it all if I were to lose my own soul** (Mark 8:36 KJ21)? And what good is it all if I am not working to have an eternal impact on my loved ones?

In the following chart you will find scriptures to reflect on (with emphasis added). Please consider how your life is in line with each of these scriptures. Go ahead and celebrate God's power and grace working through you...or you may need to consider what decisions you will have to make to more fully live out God's purpose in your life. Yes, we need daily reminders and daily intentions!

Let's make these scriptures as impactful as possible, so that we can be the "good" that our world needs and that God has intended. The first column contains scriptures about **our opportunity for eternal impact.** In the second column, please consider the scripture and rate what you feel/think is your current status on a scale of 1–5. Then, in the third column, please consider what God has said in the scripture and rate your current status on a scale of 1–5 based on how you think God would rank it.

1. My life **practically never** reflects God's will in this scripture
2. My life **rarely** reflects God's will in this scripture
3. My life **sometimes** reflects God's will in this scripture
4. My life **usually** reflects God's will in this scripture
5. My life **practically always** reflects God's will in this scripture

Our Eternal Impact	Personal Thoughts	God's Thoughts
1. **Matthew 28:18–20** – Then Jesus came to them and said, "All authority in heaven and on earth has been given to me. Therefore go and make disciples of all nations, baptizing them in the name of the Father and of the Son and of the Holy Spirit, and **teaching** them to obey everything I have commanded you. And surely I am with you always, to the very end of the age."		
2. **Matthew 5:13–16** – "**You are the salt** of the earth. But if the salt loses its saltiness, how can it be made salty again? It is no longer good for anything, except to be thrown out and trampled underfoot. **You are the light** of the world. A town built on a hill cannot be hidden. Neither do people light a lamp and put it under a bowl. Instead they put it on its stand, and it **gives light** to everyone in the house. In the same way, **let your light shine** before others, that they may see **your good deeds** and glorify your Father in heaven."		
3. **1 Peter 2:12** – **Live such good lives** among the pagans that, though they accuse you of doing wrong, they may see your **good deeds** and glorify God on the day he visits us. ESV: Keep your **conduct** among the Gentiles **honorable,** so that when they speak against you as evildoers, they may see your good deeds and glorify God on the day of visitation.		
4. **Philippians 2:13** – It is God who works in you to **will** and to **act** in order to **fulfill his good purpose.**		
5. **James 1:12** – Blessed is the one who **perseveres** under trial because, having **stood the test,** that person will receive the crown of life that the Lord has promised to those who love him.		
6. **Colossians 4:2–6** – Devote yourselves to prayer, being watchful and thankful. And **pray for us, too,** that God may		

open a door for our message, so that we may proclaim the mystery of Christ, for which I am in chains. Pray that I may proclaim it clearly, as I should. **Be wise** in the way you act toward outsiders; **make the most of every opportunity.** Let your **conversation** be always full of grace, seasoned with salt, so that you may **know** how to answer everyone.		
7. Titus 1:9 – He must **hold firmly** to the trustworthy message as it has been taught, so that he can **encourage** others by sound doctrine and refute those who oppose it.		
8. Luke 12:33–34 – Sell your possessions and **give to the poor.** Provide purses for yourselves that will not wear out, a **treasure in heaven** that will never fail, where no thief comes near and no moth destroys. For where your treasure is, there your heart will be also. **ERV:** Sell the things you have and give that money to those who need it. **This is the only way you can keep your riches from being lost.** You will be **storing treasure in heaven that lasts forever.** Thieves can't steal that treasure, and moths can't destroy it. Your heart will be where your treasure is.		
9. Matthew 24:14 – And this **gospel of the kingdom** will be **preached** in the whole world as a testimony to all nations, and then the end will come.		
10. Romans 1:1–2 – Paul, a servant of Christ Jesus, called to be an apostle and **set apart for the gospel of God**—the gospel he promised beforehand through his prophets in the Holy Scriptures.		
11. Luke 10:25–37 – On one occasion an expert in the law stood up to test Jesus. "Teacher," he asked, "what must I do to inherit eternal life?" "What is written in the Law?" he replied. "How do you read it?" He answered, **"Love the Lord your God with all your heart and with all your soul and with all your strength and with all your mind"**; and **"Love your neighbor as yourself."** "You have answered correctly," Jesus replied. "Do this and you will live." But he wanted to justify himself, so he asked Jesus, "And who is my neighbor?" In reply Jesus said: "A man was going down from Jerusalem to Jericho, when he was attacked by robbers. They stripped him of his clothes, beat him and went away, leaving him half dead. A priest happened to be going down the same road,		

and when he saw the man, he passed by on the other side. So too, a Levite, when he came to the place and saw him, passed by on the other side. **But a Samaritan,** as he traveled, came where the man was; and when he saw him, he took pity on him. He went to him and bandaged his wounds, pouring on oil and wine. Then he put the man on his own donkey, brought him to an inn and took care of him. The next day he took out two denarii and gave them to the innkeeper. 'Look after him,' he said, 'and when I return, I will reimburse you for any extra expense you may have.' Which of these three do you think was a neighbor to the man who fell into the hands of robbers?" The expert in the law replied, "The one who had mercy on him." Jesus told him, **"Go and do likewise."**		
12. **2 Timothy 2:22 – Flee** the evil desires of youth and **pursue** righteousness, faith, love and peace, **along with** those who call on the Lord out of a pure heart.		
13. **Galatians 5:1** – It is for freedom that Christ has set us free. **Stand firm,** then, and do not let yourselves be burdened again by a yoke of slavery.		
14. **1 Timothy 6:17–19** – Command those who are rich in this present world not to be arrogant nor to put their hope in wealth, which is so uncertain, but to **put their hope in God,** who richly provides us with everything for our enjoyment. Command them to do good, to be rich in **good deeds,** and to be **generous** and **willing** to share. In this way they will **lay up treasure** for themselves as a firm foundation for the coming age, so that they may **take hold of the life** that is truly **life.**		
15. **Philippians 4:8–9** – Finally, brothers and sisters, whatever is true, whatever is noble, whatever is right, whatever is pure, whatever is lovely, whatever is admirable—if anything is excellent or praiseworthy—**think about such things.** Whatever you have learned or received or heard from me, or seen in me—**put it into practice.** And the God of peace will be with you.		
16. **Ephesians 2:8–10** – For it is by grace you have been saved, through faith—and this is not from yourselves, it is the gift of God—not by works, so that no one can boast. For we are God's handiwork, created in Christ Jesus to **do good works,** which God prepared in advance for us to do.		

17. **Matthew 25:31–40** – "When the Son of Man comes in his glory, and all the angels with him, he will sit on his glorious throne. All the nations will be gathered before him, and he will separate the people one from another as a shepherd separates the sheep from the goats. He will put the sheep on his right and the goats on his left. Then the King will say to those on his right, 'Come, you who are blessed by my Father; take your inheritance, the kingdom prepared for you since the creation of the world. For I was hungry and **you gave** me something to eat, I was thirsty and **you gave** me something to drink, I was a stranger and you **invited me** in, I needed clothes and **you clothed** me, I was sick and **you looked after** me, I was in prison and **you came** to visit me.' Then the righteous will answer him, 'Lord, when did we see you hungry and feed you, or thirsty and give you something to drink? When did we see you a stranger and invite you in, or needing clothes and clothe you? When did we see you sick or in prison and go to visit you?' The King will reply, 'Truly I tell you, whatever you **did for one of the least of these brothers and sisters** of mine, you did for me.'"		
18. **Mark 16:15** – He said to them, "Go into all the world and **preach the gospel to all creation**."		

REFLECTION

1. For the scriptures above, what do you see as God's plan for your eternal impact?

_____

_____

_____

_____

_____

_____

_____

_____

2. How do these scriptures make you feel?

_____

_____

_____

_____

_____

_____

3. Are your thoughts about the scriptures on your personal impact generally positive or negative?

_____

_____

_____

_____

_____

_____

4. How will your behavior be most changed by the scriptures on your personal impact? What daily decisions and intentions will help you be more aligned to God's will for your life to the full (John 10:10) and eternal impact?

_____

_____

_____

_____

_____

_____

I totally believe that we all can reach our full potential in each area of our lives. I believe that God wants us to be excellent. We have the best model, as Jesus did everything well (Mark 7:37). As we consider all the components of our lives—professional, financial, wellness, relationships, emotional/mental and spiritual—my

question is, "What good is it?" What good will it be if we reach the height of accomplishments in our careers and professions and suffer the loss of our souls (DARBY)? What good is it if we become millionaires or billionaires and lose or forfeit our souls (NIV and KJV)? What good is it if we are in the best physical shape ever, but we forfeit our lives in the eternal kingdom of God (AMPC)? What good is it if we are considered gurus of emotional and mental health or overcome great mental health challenges and we ourselves are lost (ERV) spiritually? What good is it if we are the most popular person or if we are liked by all the "right people" or have all the "right relationships" but destroy ourselves (CEV) spiritually? And what good is it if we marry our dream partner and don't get each other to heaven—the eternal kingdom of God (AMPC)?

I had two single, male disciple clients who shared that they desperately wanted to be "successful" in life, get married, and overcome some purity issues. During the Time Line Therapy® breakthrough process we discuss values—what and who are important to the clients in their lives. Sadly, despite being disciples for years, neither of these brothers ranked God as first in their hierarchy of values. Though God, ministers, and disciples consistently talk about God being first, God was not #2 in these brothers' ranked values. Though these two brothers desired God's blessings for a spouse and though they desired to overcome consistent personal torment, God wasn't even #3 in their list of values. Though they both said they wanted to overcome their deep-rooted purity struggles, the reality was that they wanted the blessings of God without their relationship with God being first in their lives. I was a bit confused after double and triple checking their rankings of what was important. I asked, and asked, and asked yet again if they were sure their rankings were in the "right order." Neither of them realized "success" with their growth efforts and neither of them have seemed to reach their personal goals.

I am the first to be excited and to support friends and family in their efforts to expand their educational pursuits. I LOVE sports and am excited to support friends and family in physical health pursuits. I am totally excited when brothers and sisters work toward greater emotional and mental health—I can't even explain the joy I feel after seeing loved ones struggle so much and then decide to do something about their struggles. Yet what matters most is how my friends and family are doing spiritually. What matters most is how I and they are walking with God. What matters most is that we get to spend eternity together and take as many folks with us as possible. **Matthew 28:18–20 is still in the Bible.** Those scriptures on discipleship are still in the Bible. Luke 19:10 still says that Jesus came to seek and to save that which was lost. God still wants everyone to be saved (1 Timothy 2:4).

REFLECTION

5. How is God's plan for seeking and saving the lost, making disciples, and teaching them to obey showing up in your life on a weekly basis?

    _____

    _____

    _____

    _____

Mark 8:36 is amazingly powerful. Let's revisit it and consider additional translations. In the versions listed on gospel.com some renderings stand out to me:

- For what shall it profit a man if he shall gain the whole world, and lose his own **soul?** (KJ21)

- What will you gain, if you **own** the whole world but **destroy** yourself? (CEV)

- It is **worth nothing** for you to have the whole world if you yourself are **lost.** (ERV)

- Do you gain anything if you win the whole world but **lose** your life? **Of course not!** (GNT)

- It is worth nothing for a person to have the whole world, if he **loses his soul.** (ICB)

- What good can it do a man to gain the whole world **at the price** of his own soul? **What can a man offer to buy back his soul once he has lost it?** (PHILLIPS)

- What good would it do to get everything you want and **lose you,** the **real you? What could you ever trade your soul for?** (MSG)

- It is **worthless** to have the whole world if they lose their souls. (NCV)

- After all, **what use is it to** win the world and lose your life? (NTE)

- **Really,** what profit is there for you to gain the whole world **and lose yourself in the process?** (VOICE)

- For what does it profit a man, to gain the whole world, and **forfeit** his life? (WEB)

- **What good will it do a man** if he gets the whole world for himself but loses his soul? (WE)

- For what profiteth it to a man, if he **win** all the world, and **do impairing to his [own] soul?** (WYC)

REFLECTION

6. Studying a variety of translations has always been helpful for me. Which Matthew 8:36 phrases and words impacted you? What impact do you want this scripture to
have on your daily thoughts, efforts, values and priorities (what's urgent and important)?

_____

_____

_____

_____

_____

_____

_____

I'll end this chapter with a scripture that all disciples of Christ
know well. "But seek first his kingdom and his righteousness,
and all these things will be given to you as well" (Matthew 6:33).
What good is it if we are not living this scripture? How are we
helping ourselves when we or anything else is "first" in our lives
as opposed to God's kingdom and his righteousness? More impor-
tantly, how is seeking first God's kingdom and his righteousness
going for you? What does this **look, sound, and feel like** in your
life? Are you "playing full out" with and for God, righteousness,
and his kingdom? Would those who know you best say that God's
kingdom and his righteousness are your first priority? Would God
say that he and righteousness are first in your life? God has given
us his all: his love, grace, Holy Spirit power, sacrifices, goodness,
holiness, hope, and his Son! As my dear friend Natacha Pierre frequently says when she talks about John 10:10, God definitely de-
serves our all, even though that will look different depending on
the day, week, month, or year. Whatever our capacity today, let's
allow God to fully work through us and our lives, especially since
we know that he is so good to us—all the time!

An unmarried woman or virgin is concerned about the Lord's affairs: Her aim is to be devoted to the Lord in both body and spirit. But a married woman is concerned about the affairs of this world—how she can please her husband. I am saying this for your own good, not to restrict you, but that you may live in a right way in undivided devotion to the Lord. (1 Corinthians 7:34–35)

REFLECTION

7. Please think through and write down your thoughts on/ responses to the questions in the last paragraph.

_____

_____

_____

_____

_____

_____

_____

_____

_____

• Chapter Nine •

God's Grace Meets Our Needs

Three times I pleaded with the Lord to take it away from me. But he said to me, "My grace is sufficient for you, for my power is made perfect in weakness." Therefore I will boast all the more gladly about my weaknesses, so that Christ's power may rest on me. That is why, for Christ's sake, I delight in weaknesses, in insults, in hardships, in persecutions, in difficulties. For when I am weak, then I am strong. (2 Corinthians 12:8-10)

I have been a baptized disciple since 1986 and have been a part of several fellowships as I went to graduate school (a few times) and took jobs in a few different cities. I have experienced and seen tons. One reason that I am writing this book is because I know that for many single sisters and brothers, being single has been a heart-wrenching disappointment and struggle. Many brothers and sisters have dreamed and planned to be married and have a family for five, ten, twenty, or even thirty years...without their dreams and plans becoming a reality. Some are "single again"; some have lost their partners to divorce. Some have even more grief as their partner for many years has passed. Many brothers and sisters have experienced chronic, cumulative, prolonged, and disenfranchised grief because they are still single. I feel for all my single friends and clients who deal with disappointment and even disillusionment with regard to their relationship status. Though all our experiences may look, sound, and feel different, it makes sense that singles can at times feel shame, sadness, hurt, worry, and even anger about our relationship status. I hope that when we do feel those things, we have loved ones around us who express their love and validate our feelings. You are not alone!

Here are just some of the reasons why singles have found their single relationship status to be challenging:

- Feeling lonely or alone
- Married culture in our world, country, and church
- Media messages that one is not "complete" without being in a relationship
- No one to go on vacation with
- Issues with roommates
- Family pressure and inquiries about our "love life"
- Desire for a family
- Covering all financial expenses alone (vs. with a partner)
- Limited/no ministry career opportunities
- Dismissal of spirituality
- Dismissal of adulthood (infantilizing)
- Diminished respect in career
- Attending work events solo
- Holidays—especially Valentine's Day
- Special events (weddings, family gatherings, etc.)
- Desire for the intimacy of a best friend
- Desire for a sexual relationship
- Sexual/biological drive
- Struggles with sexual purity
- Desire for a greater sense of belonging
- Support when needing care (sick, emergencies, etc.)
- Empty home at the beginning and end of the days
- Feeling "unwanted," not chosen

- Risk in pursuing a possible interest
- Believing that marriage is "the promised land"
- Believing that marriage is easy or that couples have a "perfect" marriage
- Accusations of unrealistic expectations or sin ("You're too picky," "You're just selfish," etc.) despite having no recommendations for potential dates or singles to consider for a relationship
- Failed relationships (we live in a fallen world – Ephesians 6:11)

REFLECTION

1. Which of the above reasons why being single is challenging resonate with you?

_____

_____

_____

_____

_____

_____

2. What would you add to the list?

_____

_____

_____

_____

_____

3. How does God want us to handle these challenges? What scriptures come to mind?

_____

_____

_____

_____

_____

I am sure that you could add to the list of why it can be very tough being single. For some singles, it may even feel traumatic thinking through that list along with the negative emotions (like anger, sadness/grief, fear/worry/anxiety, hurt and guilt/shame) and limiting beliefs attached to your experiences. I thought that I would have a family in my twenties. I am now fifty-four years old. I always wanted to be married and have a child, especially since the "Jones bloodline" will end with me...on both my mother's and father's side. I even had to grieve not taking advantage of saving my eggs (for a future pregnancy) before there was no longer an opportunity to do so. I share all of that to say that our emotions are frequently valid, appropriate, and warranted. We need to validate our emotions and have friends who do the same. We are not alone in our unfulfilled desires and the resulting grief.

The human reality is that we are made for relationships (Genesis 2:18). God wants a connection with us, and we can be an expression of his love in our connections with others. This has been a problem for humankind and for disciples—single and married. I believe another reality is that, as a minister once told me, relationships are the hardest thing we do. As a coach and licensed counselor, I have seen countless people with relationship or social challenges. I have seen disciples come into the fellowship without ever having had healthy relationships. Sadly, there sometimes seems to be an expectation that people will all of a sudden (after baptism) know how to have healthy relationships. As I mentioned before, our behavior is largely fueled by our subconscious internal representations, our emotions, and our physiology (NLP Communication Model – Chapter 5). To have healthy relationships, we need to have healthy levels of self-awareness, self-management, social awareness, and relationship management skills. We need healthy EQ. Since my book, *Spiritual Transformation: Emotional Intelligence and Freedom,* extensively addresses EQ, I won't go into further details here.

I will share the following scriptures as encouragement. At the same time, in no way would I ever want to invalidate anyone's emotions and grief about being single. There is too much pressure to be "hitched" or coupled in our culture. In fact, to my father, I don't think it mattered much who I married; he just wanted me to be married. It seemed that he considered being single as a defect of some sort. I also know that he wanted me to be happy and wanted me to have what I wanted—a loving and spiritual family. He was aware of the grief I experienced regarding my relationship status. God is the best father we could ever ask for, and here is some of what our Father says:

John 16:33

"I have told you these things, so that in me you may have peace. In this world you will have trouble. But take heart! I have overcome the world."

2 Corinthians 12:8–10

Three times I pleaded with the Lord to take it away from me. But he said to me, "My grace is sufficient for you, for my power is made perfect in weakness." Therefore I will boast all the more gladly about my weaknesses, so that Christ's power may rest on me. That is why, for Christ's sake, I delight in weaknesses, in insults, in hardships, in persecutions, in difficulties. For when I am weak, then I am strong.

Philippians 4:8–9

Finally, brothers and sisters, whatever is true, whatever is noble, whatever is right, whatever is pure, whatever is lovely, whatever is admirable—if anything is excellent or praiseworthy—think about such things. Whatever you have learned or received or heard from me, or seen in me—put it into practice. And the God of peace will be with you.

Jeremiah 9:24

But let the one who boasts boast about this:
that they have the understanding to know me,
that I am the Lord, who exercises kindness,
justice and righteousness on earth,
for in these I delight,"
declares the Lord.

Romans 8:28

And we know that in all things God works for the good of those who love him, who have been called according to his purpose.

1 Corinthians 13:13

And now these three remain: faith, hope and love. But the greatest of these is love.

John 10:27–29

"My sheep listen to my voice; I know them, and they follow me. I give them eternal life, and they shall never perish; no one will snatch them out of my hand. My Father, who has given them to me, is greater than all; no one can snatch them out of my Father's hand."

REFLECTION

4. Which of these scriptures resonate with you? Which of the scriptures encourage you? Which scriptures can help you focus on what matters most to God?

_____

_____

_____

_____

_____

_____

We can live in a state of sulk because we do not have what we want in regard to our relationship status, or we can rely on God's grace and work to consciously and subconsciously be aligned with Philippians 4. We can decide to wire and fire (in our neural pathways/connections) either the thoughts that lead to depression or the thoughts that lead to joy. And, in case you need a bit of support, here's a list of just some of the reasons **why singles have found their relationship status to be awesome, satisfying, rewarding, fun, enjoyable, and fulfilling:**

- Totally in charge of our own personal happiness and well-being
- Time to solidify personal values (spiritual, emotional, physical, and social) and mission statement
- Time to develop a healthy sense of self—value, worth, esteem
- Time to focus on investing in relationship with God (undivided devotion) (Jeremiah 9:24)
- Time to focus on the Great Commission (Matthew 28:18–20)
- Time to develop personal contentment—enjoying our own company
- Freedom and flexibility—time, routines, decisions, finances, etc.
- Can choose to save money (for a house, car, retirement, investments, long-term care, etc.)
- Time to build great, rich relationships (family, friends, professional network, etc.)
- More time for rest and relaxation (mentally, emotionally, physically)
- More mental space

- Time to get healthier spiritually, emotionally, physically, and socially—personal development and self-care
- Time to develop relationship management skills (emotional intelligence)
- Time to focus on education and career goals
- Higher levels of creativity and intimacy in friendships (scientifically)
- Time to travel
- Time to serve others (fellow disciples, widows, children, the poor, and the community)
- Time to enjoy healthy solitude
- Time to get to know a variety of other singles
- Evading the troubles of marriage (1 Corinthians 7:28)
- Having a bed to yourself—sleeping more soundly
- Setting your home thermostat at your desired/needed temperature
- Evading the insane divorce rate and prevalence of loneliness in marriages
- Eating what you want when you want to
- Watching what you want when you want to (TV, movies, etc.)

We can focus on the first list, invest emotional energy there, allow that list to be the narrative of our lives, and live as victims... or we can decide to rely on God's grace to live John 10:10—a life to the full. Let's deal with our grief in healthy ways (research and connect with a professional counselor/coach if you need to) and make the most of our opportunities where God has planted us! God's grace truly is sufficient.

REFLECTION

5. In which list does your mind typically reside—the challenges of being single or the blessings of being single? Which thoughts are you typically wiring and firing together? How has that been helpful or harmful?

    _____

    _____

    _____

    _____

    _____

    _____

6. On which list will you choose to focus each day? Why?

    _____

    _____

    _____

    _____

    _____

    _____

7. What does God desire for your mindset and life?

    _____

    _____

    _____

    _____

    _____

Chapter Ten

Our Brainpower—Creating Life to the Full

If you think you can, or if you think you can't, you're right.
—*Henry Ford*

Where there is no vision, the people perish.
—Proverbs 29:18 KJ21

In *Breaking the Habit of Being Yourself: How to Lose Your Mind and Create a New One*, Dr. Joe Dispenza (2017, p. xxi) notes, "The latest research supports the notion that we have a natural ability to change the brain and body by thought alone." Dr. Dispenza is an expert in neuroscience, neurology, the mind and body connection, epigenetics, and quantum physics. He has also studied brain function and chemistry, cellular biology, memory formation, aging, and longevity. After my postgraduate NLP and Time Line Therapy® training (in 2018) and after reading some of Dr. Dispenza's resources, I hope and plan to participate in one of his workshops when time allows. **What we receive and achieve is directly connected to what we perceive, conceive, and believe.**

Also, in one of his many interviews, Dr. Dispenza discusses how we create our state of being (Jay Shetty Instagram post, n.d.):

Thoughts are the vocabulary of the brain. Feelings are the vocabulary of your body. **How you think and how you feel creates your state of being.** So then, if you wake up in the morning and you come back to your senses with a clean slate and you say, "I don't feel anything," you say, "Let me think about all the problems in my life." Well, all those problems are connected to different people or different objects and things at different times and places. The moment you remember your problems a memory is a record of the past. You are thinking in the past. Every one of those problems have an emotion associated with it. So all of a sudden you feel unhappy, you feel bitter, you feel frustrated. So now your body is in the past. **So then, most people then create a state of being that's connected to their past and if they are in the familiar past, then they are going to create the predictable future and they are going to fall back into routine.**

REFLECTION

1. How have you seen your thinking/perceiving and vision (or lack thereof) impact your state of being and your life?

    _____

    _____

    _____

    _____

    _____

    _____

In my coaching practice, I have seen incredible mental and emotional transformations with the use of NLP and Time Line Therapy® techniques. I previously listed the most common "greater problems" that clients have eliminated (Chapter 6). Yes, eliminated! The Time Line Therapy® breakthrough process allows us to clean up our past and eliminate emotional and mental baggage. Recall that in one demonstration, when I was first introduced to

Time Line Therapy® techniques, **I no longer believed that I was not good enough.** That thought that dogged me my entire life just didn't make sense anymore! In just a few minutes, my neural circuitry had been rewired. It's such an incredible feeling mentally and emotionally to no longer carry the baggage of negative emotions and limiting beliefs connected to past events. Time Line Therapy® is my all-time favorite therapeutic modality, as with my logical, results- and math-oriented brain, I enjoy seeing amazing, efficient, and effective results and transformations.

I no longer enjoy working only with psychological treatments that focus on our conscious mind and coping skills. I would rather have clients invest in therapies that transform our lives in the greatest way possible, in our subconscious minds. Let alone the fact that our unconscious programming drives about 95 percent of what happens in our lives. Just as it is hard to describe to someone the life of a disciple without them seeing and living it, I have not been able to find words that sufficiently describe the impact that Time Line Therapy® has had on my life and the miracles I witness with clients. A few clients have "Success Stories" videos on my website (www.cresendajones.com), but there is nothing like seeing and feeling your own subconscious transformation!

One of the techniques that Master Time Line Therapy® Practitioners are trained to use is called Creating Your Future®. The purpose of this technique is to bring our dreams into reality as we access our subconscious minds. I am sure that you've been encouraged to visualize success before you attempt to reach a desired goal or outcome. **Visualization** is highly powerful, and the Tad James Creating Your Future® technique is even more impactful. This and the other techniques can create powerful change in every area of a person's life. As many have noted, the universe will deliver what we want. You may have heard of the **law of attraction** or may have even felt it in your own life or seen it in others:

- Knowing that with God there is abundance, and it leads to us having all that we need
- Self-sabotaging thoughts becoming a reality

- Visualization of a goal leading to fruition
- Thinking that you will fail, and it leads to failure
- Knowing that you will succeed, and it leads to success
- Knowing that you have enough time, reducing anxiety and increasing focus
- Knowing that humans make mistakes, reducing the need for perfectionism, etc.
- Knowing that God's got you and loves you providing the peace that passes understanding
- Visualization of an effective presentation, resulting in a successful meeting and discussion
- Thinking that that sister or brother will never be interested in you, and it leads to exactly that happening
- Ruminating on loneliness, and you miss out on opportunities for connection
- Setting and focusing on your SMART goals, and they become a reality
- Thinking that you don't have enough (money, education, intelligence, spirituality, self-control, etc.), resulting in you not having enough
- Thinking happy thoughts, leading to you feeling happy (Philippians 4)
- Having a bad attitude about someone, leading to difficult interactions
- Concentrating on your desired outcome, and it materializes

REFLECTION

2. How have you seen the law of attraction work in your life—negatively and positively?

----

3. What negative emotions, limiting beliefs, and greater problem would you like to delete from your subconscious mind?

We can use visualization and our thoughts to attract the things we want. We can put a goal out into our future so that it actually happens. After we have subconsciously cleaned up our past, we can then program our Time Line (how we store and organize our memories internally) for future success. Cleaning up our past means that we eliminate negative emotions connected to past events so that there are no conflicts between the past and our future goals. We can change our mental state from being full of doubt and faithlessness to one of trusting God's goodness and love. We can even change our moods. We can fix our attention on our desired state, as Philippians 4 commands us. It is so cool that God's commands are always about our good (Romans 8:28)!

If you get nothing else out of this book and chapter, I hope you get this: **Every thought we think, every action, every deed creates results** both directly and indirectly (James, 2009, p. 69). Tad and Adriana James (2009) note that "the mind always produces results exactly according to your instructions. If your thinking and goals aren't aligned, your thinking will win out." If we wish to have the life to the full, we need to make it our dream to have God's life to the full! It requires that we change our thought processes; we must direct our focus so that it is only on what we want and desire (p. 125).

The Time Line Therapy® breakthrough process (developed by Tad James) calls us to visualize and consequently "create our future." 1 Peter 1:13 tells us to prepare our minds for action (ESV) and that our minds must be clear and ready for action (GW). To support this change requisite, clients are taken through a technique by which a specific goal is inserted, at the unconscious level, in their future Time Line. With this creative visualization, clients also reevaluate all events between the current moment and their future goal to ensure that their goal is supported. The unconscious mind will then look for ways to support the goal. Tony Robbins says that **80 percent of success in anything is psychological and the remaining 20 percent is mechanics** (Mann, n.d.).

It is amazing that God created us so that our mind does not distinguish between something we vividly imagine and something we experience. **Our brain does not know the difference between reality and imagination.** Napoleon Hill reportedly said, "Whatever the mind of man can conceive and believe, it can achieve." Perhaps that is one reason why there are many scriptures that address where our thoughts need to be. Thus, we can capitalize on God's design of our brains so that we can create the amazing future that we envision and that he desires for us!

The Creating Our Future® technique is an easy process using advanced mental technologies. Once this technique is completed, the client knows (especially subconsciously) what they need to do to get what they want. For us, that is God's life to the full (John 10:10). During the technique, the client creates new memories for their future Time Line. If you do not have access to a Time Line Therapy® breakthrough process, which rewires neural pathways at the subconscious level, there are great resources that help us to take captive our conscious thoughts.

In *Spiritual Transformation,* I discuss valuable information about how you can "Master Your Mind" in Chapter 4, which includes detailed information regarding:

1. Our Brain, Personality, and Emotions
2. The NLP Model of Communication
3. We Feel It First – The Physical Pathway for EQ
4. The Power of Our Neuroplastic Brain
5. Our Conscious and Unconscious Minds
6. Brain Waves
7. Paul's Comments on Our Brains
8. The Brain and Our Relationships

Then in Chapters 9 and 10 the following are considered:

1. Time Line Therapy® – Transforming Our Neurology
2. God's Word on Transformation
3. Three Requisites for Mind Changes & Soul Transformations
4. Taking Radical Action

REFLECTION

4. Considering that God has called us to love him with all our minds (Luke 10:27), how much do you think or feel you know about your brain?

_____

_____

_____

_____

Cognitive Behavior Therapy Resources

While Time Line Therapy® rewires our neural pathways in our subconscious minds, Cognitive Behavior Therapy (CBT) works with our conscious thoughts. CBT is the most popular therapeutic modality used by licensed therapists. It is very easy to find a wealth of information on CBT with an internet search and through contact with any counselor. If you cannot access Time Line Therapy®, which heals on a subconscious level, it is still very helpful to use CBT principles to develop coping skills and work on increasing awareness and the health of your thinking patterns. As you have already seen in the NLP Communication Model (Chapter 5 in this book and Chapter 4 in *Spiritual Transformation*), our thoughts and feelings lead to our behavior.

Even after clients finish the Time Line Therapy® breakthrough process in which they experience healing, some who have not developed healthy coping skills are referred to talk therapy for these needs. With all the amazing and practical spiritual food we receive, I believe that many disciples can effectively apply CBT principles on their own. To that end, I am including references to some helpful CBT worksheets for your use. If you find that you are not able to realize your desired emotional/mental health outcomes, please work with a licensed professional.

Since TherapistAid.com has copyrighted materials, please access their website (https://www.therapistaid.com/therapy-work-sheets/cbt/none#) and review the worksheets and handouts on the following topics:

1. What Are Core Beliefs?

2. The Cognitive Model

3. The Cognitive Triangle

4. The Cognitive Model (Example Sheet and Practice Sheet)

5. Automatic Thoughts

6. Cognitive Distortions

7. Challenging Negative Thoughts

Many more CBT resources are included on this website (and countless others). When the skills discussed in the handouts are accessed and implemented, CBT has been found to be helpful with support for success and numerous emotional and mental health challenges.

REFLECTION

5. Because of the weekly Bible messages we hear and the conscious, mindful decisions we have made in our walks with God, we may have a bit of an advantage regarding using our brainpower. How can you further use CBT skills to optimize your brainpower as you strive for John 10:10's life to the full?

   _____

   _____

   _____

   _____

   _____

   _____

What Can You Do Now?

If you are like me, you want to act on the things you read about so that you can mitigate anything in your life that is unhelpful and live life to the full with God and your loved ones. A recent client had an unbelievable transformation when they implemented a **daily morning routine** that my NLP trainers shared. It is also what I ask clients to do as we work together through the Time Line Therapy® breakthrough process or the Mastering Emotional Intelligence® workshop based on *Emotional Intelligence 2.0*. After paying $7,000 to learn how to facilitate the workshop and taking the Bradberry and Greaves EQ Appraisal®, I learned that what would improve my EQ the most is Breathing Right. In addition to our vital daily time with God, I need to consistently do these four things, along with you!

I. **Breathe Right** – As noted in *Emotional Intelligence 2.0*, most of us take shallow breaths throughout our day and do not fully contract our diaphragm in order to fill our lungs. We harm our brains when we are not breathing effectively. Our stomach needs to expand, or we are not getting the oxygen that is needed to our brains. The 4-7-8 breathing technique has been found to be helpful. Just inhale (through your nose) for the count of four, hold your breath for the count of seven, and exhale (through your mouth) for the count of eight. Doing at least four cycles each morning is helpful. Doing this throughout your day, and especially if you are feeling any stress or anxiety, is beneficial.

2. **Consider Gratitude** – Before clients have their first appointment for the Time Line Therapy® breakthrough process, I require that they journal for at least five consecutive days. One portion of the journaling entails writing down four things for which they are grateful. To optimize the practice of gratitude, my NLP trainers Steph and Shay Schafeitel recommend that we close our eyes, put our hands over our hearts and really feel the gratitude. I typically pray to bask in God's grace as much as possible. We also need to bask in gratitude every day!

3. **Visualize Goals** – When visualizing something that we plan to accomplish today (this week, month or year), for it to be most effective, the Creating Your Future® technique instructs us to consider what the last step of accomplishing the goal will be. What will be happening when you know you have achieved your desired outcome or goal? What will you hear, see, and feel when you know you have achieved your goal? Make a picture/movie of that last step and soak it all in! Make the picture/movie have the best feelings, sounds, and visuals you can imagine. Sit with that picture/movie and all the great feelings. Then, step out of the picture/movie and imagine that you see yourself in the picture/movie accomplishing your goal. As with the Breathe Right exercise, energize this picture/movie with four deep breaths and the faith that you will achieve your goal and have the necessary accompanying deeds (James 2:20–26). Do this visualization exercise as much as need-

ed, but at least once a day!

4. **Meditate** – Both breathing correctly and visualizing goals can be considered part of meditation, yet meditation can go beyond those two actions. Wikipedia (n.d.) notes that meditation "is a practice in which an individual uses a technique—such as mindfulness, or focusing the mind on a particular object, thought, or activity—to train attention and awareness, and achieve a mentally clear and emotionally calm and stable state." The emotional and physical benefits of meditation are widely known and discussed. This practice can lead to increased and more effective self-awareness, stress management, focus, creativity, patience, emotional regulation, compassion, and tolerance. With meditation, our perspectives can get more aligned with God's, and we can reduce the impact of negative emotions (like anger, sadness/grief, fear/worry/anxiety, hurt, guilt/shame) and even physical pain.

Just as these four actions have transformed my clients, you too can use your brainpower to more fully live life! I am very grateful for all that I learned in my NLP and Time Line Therapy® practitioner and master trainings and from those in the various fields of neurology. I hope, pray, and know that you can and will use your brainpower (starting now) to more fruitfully walk with God and walk in the fullness of all that he has planned for you. Let's win this spiritual battle and take as many loved ones as possible with us to the Great Banquet (Luke 14)!

REFLECTION

6. How conscious are you of your breathing practices? Do you have healthy breathing practices? Why is breathing important for your ability to optimize your brainpower and more fruitfully walk in John 10:10?

_____

_____

_____

_____

_____

_____

7. Once again, because of our daily talks (prayers) with God, we may have a bit of a head start on meditating in gratitude on a consistent basis. How has daily gratitude impacted your state of being (spiritually, mentally, emotionally, socially, and biologically)?

_____

_____

_____

_____

_____

_____

_____

8. What spiritual, mental, emotional, health, social, and physical goals would you like to visualize and manifest in your life as you work toward manifesting John 10:10 all the more in your life?

_____

_____

_____

_____

_____

_____

_____

Chapter Eleven

Think on These Things —Philippians 4

Is being single easy? No. Is being married easy? No. Is life easy? No. Is being in jail easy? No. Paul was in prison or on house arrest when he wrote the letter to the disciples in Philippi. I am guessing that no one is imprisoned while you are reading this book—if so, I'd happily become one of your pen pals! The reality is that we will have trouble in this world: "I have told you these things, so that in me you may have peace. In this world you will have trouble. But take heart! I have overcome the world" (John 16:33). God knows that we are dealing with spiritual forces of evil (Ephesians 6:12) and that we need our full armor every day in order to take our stand against Satan's schemes (Ephesians 6:11). We must not only take our stand spiritually; we must also take our stand mentally. We need our mindpower armor! God, through Paul, commands us to be healthy in our thoughts and mind!

In Philippians 4:4–9, Paul gives his final exhortations as he states:

Rejoice in the Lord always. I will say it again: Rejoice! Let your gentleness be evident to all. The Lord is near. Do not be anxious about anything, but in every situation, by prayer and petition, with thanksgiving, present your requests to God. And the peace of God, which transcends all understanding, will guard your hearts and your minds in Christ Jesus.

Finally, brothers and sisters, whatever is true, whatever is noble, whatever is right, whatever is pure, whatever is lovely, whatever is admirable—if anything

is excellent or praiseworthy—think about such things.
Whatever you have learned or received or heard from me, or
seen in me—put it into practice. And the God of peace will be
with you. (emphasis added)

In many ways, **we determine our current and future life by what we decide to think about.** In love, God helps us out with how to guard our hearts and minds. He tells us what to think about. I have included synonyms for the words Paul uses in Philippians 4—whatever is:

1. **True** – pure, accurate, authentic, bona fide, sincere, correct, perfect, honest, legitimate, proper, truthful

2. **Noble** – benevolent, brilliant, charitable, dignified, extraordinary, grand, great, honorable, humane, magnificent, splendid, virtuous, worthy, high-minded

3. **Right** – fair, just, appropriate, good, honest, proper, suitable, true, accurate, precise, correct, perfect, sure, valid

4. **Pure** – authentic, clean, uncontaminated, purified, refined, unadulterated, wholesome, immaculate, spotless, unblemished, unpolluted, unsoiled

5. **Lovely** – alluring, beautiful, captivating, charming, delicate, delicious, delightful, enchanting, exquisite, gorgeous, graceful, pleasant, pleasing, splendid, stunning, sweet

6. **Admirable** – commendable, excellent, laudable, valuable, wonderful, rare, solid, meritorious, deserving, estimable, copacetic

7. **Excellent** – accomplished, admirable, distinguished, exceptional, exemplary, exquisite, first-rate, great, magnificent, outstanding, skillful, sterling, superb, superlative

8. **Praiseworthy** – commendable, creditable, honorable, laudable, exemplary, salt of the earth, stellar, worthy

Those words are exceedingly powerful! Especially if we keep our minds on such things. Those are just the words from a thesaurus; additional words found in various translations of God's word for the things on which we need to keep our minds focused include: of good report, of virtue, confirmed by God's word, of moral excellence, holy, kind, lovable, friendly, worthwhile, amiable, modest, of good fame, praise of discipline, respected, acceptable, excellence of character, gracious, of good repute, belonging to love, upright, attractive, straight, clean, brings praise to God, sooth, chaste, and grave. God instructs us to keep in mind any praise!

Furthermore, the following versions are too unique and encouraging to not fully include here in our effort to understand what God wants in our lives:

- *Finally, believers, whatever is true, whatever is honorable and worthy of respect, whatever is right and confirmed by God's word, whatever is pure and wholesome, whatever is lovely and brings peace, whatever is admirable and of good repute; if there is any excellence, if there is anything worthy of praise, think continually on these things [center your mind on them, and implant them in your heart]. (AMP)*

- *For the rest, brethren, whatever is true, whatever is worthy of reverence and is honorable and seemly, whatever is just, whatever is pure, whatever is lovely and lovable, whatever is kind and winsome and gracious, if there is any virtue and excellence, if there is anything worthy of praise, think on and weigh and take account of these things [fix your minds on them]. (AMPC)*

- *Here is a last piece of advice. If you believe in goodness and if you value the approval of God, fix your minds on the things which are holy and right and pure and beautiful and good. Model your conduct on what you have learned from me, on what I have told you and shown you, and you*

> *will find the God of peace will be with you. (PHILLIPS)*
>
> - *And now, brothers, as I close this letter, let me say this one more thing: Fix your thoughts on what is true and good and right. Think about things that are pure and lovely, and dwell on the fine, good things in others. Think about all you can praise God for and be glad about. (TLB)*
>
> - *Summing it all up, friends, I'd say you'll do best by filling your minds and meditating on things true, noble, reputable, authentic, compelling, gracious—the best, not the worst; the beautiful, not the ugly; things to praise, not things to curse. Put into practice what you learned from me, what you heard and saw and realized. Do that, and God, who makes everything work together, will work you into his most excellent harmonies. (MSG)*
>
> - *Christian brothers, keep your minds thinking about whatever is true, whatever is respected, whatever is right, whatever is pure, whatever can be loved, and whatever is well thought of. If there is anything good and worth giving thanks for, think about these things. (NLV)*
>
> - *Furthermore, brethren, whatever things are true, whatever things are honourable, whatever things are just, whatever things are pure, whatever things belong to love, whatever things are of good report, if there be any virtuous thing, if there be any praiseworthy thing: these same have in your minds. (NMB)*

Lastly, the command to **"think about such things"** in the NIV has some very helpful variations in other translations: think on these things; dwell on these things; focus your thoughts on these things; keep your minds on; don't ever stop thinking about; fill your minds with; keep your thoughts on; continue to think about the things; exercise yourselves in these things; fix your thoughts on; let your mind dwell on; let your minds be filled with; always think about; think about those kinds of things; meditate on these things; keep you minds thinking about; be considering these things; think on and weigh on; and these are the things you should think through.

REFLECTION

1. Which translations of words and phrases in Philippians 4 help you to most understand where God wants us to place our thoughts? Feel free to choose your favorites and write your own version of Philippians 4:8.

_____

_____

_____

_____

_____

_____

God only wants what is best for us. He wants us to have life to the full! He is completely gracious and the best teacher we could ever desire. If you are not yet convinced about the power of our minds and thoughts, here are just a few more scriptures (with emphasis added) to meditate on, study, and integrate into your life:

Deuteronomy 30:19 NLT

*Today I have given you the choice between life and death, between blessings and curses. Now I call on heaven and earth to witness the choice you make. Oh, that you would **choose life,** so that you and your descendants might live!*

Romans 12:2 NLT

*Don't copy the behavior and customs of this world, but let God transform you into a new person by **changing the way you think.** Then you will learn to know God's will for you, which is good and pleasing and perfect.*

2 Timothy 1:7 NLT

> *God has not given us a spirit of fear and timidity, but of pow-er, love, and **self-discipline.***

Exodus 34:7 NLT

> *I lavish unfailing love to a thousand generations.*
>> *I forgive iniquity, rebellion, and sin.*
> *But I do not excuse the guilty.*
>> *I lay the sins of the parents up on their children and grandchildren;*
> *the entire family is affected—*
>> *even children in the third and fourth **generations.***

2 Corinthians 10:5

> *We **demolish** arguments and every pretension that sets itself up against the knowledge of God, and we **take captive every thought** to make it obedient to Christ.*

Psalm 46:10

> ***Be still, and know** that I **am** God.*

Proverbs 23:7 NASB

> ***As he thinks** within himself, so he is.*

REFLECTION

2. Which verses help you to understand how important our thinking, attitudes, and focus and the resulting behaviors are to God?

_____

_____

_____

_____

_____

_____

_____

Let's trust God regarding what is good for us spiritually and mentally. Let's devote ourselves to thinking "about such things" as much as possible. Let's devote ourselves to realizing the life to the full (John 10:10) that God has planned for each and every one of us—a life of spiritual and mental peace and blessings. *Carpe diem!*

• Chapter Twelve •

Testimonies

Just in case you are tempted to think otherwise, I wanted to make it clear that I have not "arrived." In this book, I am sharing things that have been tremendously transformative and helpful for me in my efforts to walk closely with God and honor him with my life. I am a sinner in need of God's forgiveness just like everyone else. I love to share what has been helpful for me. I also LOVE to hear great news and encouragement from my fellow disciples and partners in the gospel. In the pages that follow, you will read about some of your brothers and sisters who are determined to live life to the full (John 10:10). They too are imperfect, and they too need God's grace. My hope is that you will know that you are not alone and that you will gain encouragement from their testimonies just as I have.

1. Priscilla Ojeda: Precious and Honored in His Sight

2. Derick Stone: Life to the Full after Divorce

3. Michelle Wright: Working and Playing Full Out

4. Courtney Wacker: Emotional Health and Social Justice

5. Peter Awolumate: Missions and Cultures

6. Melika Miller: Dreaming and Trusting God

7. Michele Smith: The Value of Being Intentional

8. Ivette Brito: "Do It Afraid"

9. Danial Naqashi: Journey with Jesus

10. Irene Umaña Lindo: Loss and Continued Service

11. Wendy Walker-Drakes: Enjoying a Second Spring

12. Dana Wynne: From Basketball to God

Priscilla Ojeda's Testimony:
Precious and Honored in His Sight
—Palm Beach Church of Christ, Florida

I grew up in the church. My dad is the lead evangelist at the Palm Beach Church (Florida). Growing up, I knew Jesus' love for me, and I knew he died on the cross for me, but I was curious as to why he loves me. Why would he die on the cross for me? So I decided to study the Bible. I was thirteen years old, and after two months of learning and diving into Scripture, I was baptized. That truly was the best day of my life. Being baptized at such a young age, I learned and grew in my reverence for God and continually dove into who Jesus is. This is where my journey of living life to the fullest spiritually started. To me, living life to the fullest spiritually is living a life in which we can grow in our relationship with God and get to know who Jesus is while showing that to others. Living life to the full is also living with freedom, being free from the chains of sin. That freedom is a gift from God to us. Being baptized at such a young age saved me from a lot of sin and heartache, and it also taught me that fulfillment only comes from God.

Growing up in the church, I knew the do's and don'ts, but just knowing those things would not help me have deep convictions or grow in my relationship with God. Something that helps me live my life to the fullest spiritually is not seeing God as just our King but as our soulmate as well. When we see God as our soulmate, we are able to have a deeper friendship with him. One thing that helped me get there is journaling and finding one scripture that makes me feel close to God.

"Do not fear, for I have redeemed you;
  I have summoned you by name; you are mine.
When you pass through the waters,
  I will be with you;
and when you pass through the rivers,
  they will not sweep over you.
When you walk through the fire,
  you will not be burned;
  the flames will not set you ablaze.
For I am the LORD your God,
  the Holy one of Israel, your Savior...
Since you are precious and honored in my sight,
  and because I love you." (Isaiah 43:1–4)

This scripture has really brought me comfort in times of questioning, hardships, or feeling like God is not with me. Having a scripture like this to go back to is super important and brings the reassurance of how much God loves you.

Dating in God's kingdom has also taught me about living life to the full spiritually. After dating for a year and a half, I am now engaged to my best friend. Dating is amazing but challenging. Living life to the full spiritually in dating is glorifying God, giving the blessings he gave you, and using it for his glory. This is not always easy, because dating does expose where we are in our relationship with God. It has exposed how I can have unrealistic expectations of people that only God can fill. It has exposed how easily I can get comfortable. It has also exposed how I can want things my way instead of listening. Dating has taught me that only God can fulfill the desire of our hearts if we seek him. Seeking God means being intentional with him and letting him lead and guide us.

Lastly, I have found that to live life to the full spiritually, it is helpful to have spiritual advice. On this great journey I have been on, there have been many advisors who have helped me along the way. Life to the full should be full of spiritual advice from those you trust and admire.

Derick Stone's Testimony:
Life to the Full after Divorce
—Louisville Church of Christ, Kentucky

I am grateful for the healing God has given me. But it hasn't been without work. I understand that time alone doesn't heal people. Time lessened the pain a bit, but it's been more what I did with that time during the healing process that helped me heal much better. It required lots of prayer, understanding God's vision for my life (as it is) through his word, and doing the self-care work. I also have children who live with me, so it's important that they see "All things are possible for one who believes" (Mark 9:23 ESV). I use all the spiritual resources around me to help me reflect, heal, grow, and re-envision what God may have for the rest of my Christ-centered life. I have a village of spiritual men I surround myself with. They pour into me and allow me to be me. I lean heavily on God's promises, like "Never will I leave you; never will I forsake you" (Hebrews 13:5) and "Cast all your anxiety on him because he cares for you" (1 Peter 5:7). I remind myself of God's presence daily when I doubt.

Physical activities also help me keep my mind busy to avoid the temptations the world throws my way. I exercise. I may do cardio and/or light weight training. I also started taking guitar lessons. I am making time to do things I felt I had no time to do when I was married. I do realize I could have been doing these things all along, but they certainly help now. I also do activities with my young daughters like roller skating or going to the park. These are small things, yet they remind us how blessed we really are despite the circumstances. Another thing that is very important is making time to have adult conversations and interactions with like-minded brothers and sisters. It is healthy and necessary to build friendships to forge the path ahead. It's a new time, a new day, and a new life. I must be willing to put my faith where my mouth is and build new friendships. And it's been great so far.

Lastly, I feel that my life is full because I attend weekly church fellowship. When I worship and reflect on the cross of Christ, my reality is checked and my perspective is challenged in that, for all I have been through, I have not yet resisted to the point of shedding my blood (Hebrews 12:4). Jesus went all the way to the cross for my sins when I was at my worst. And no matter what I have endured, I have not endured what he did. That encourages me to persevere, to endure, because if Jesus was crucified for me, I can run this race for him. I can and will overcome and be victorious.

Michelle Wright's Testimony:
Working and Playing Full Out
—North River Church of Christ, Georgia

In John 10:10, Jesus is quoted as saying that he came so that we may have life and have it to the full. I'm sure the meaning of this statement has been debated and analyzed for millennia, and I'm not here to give a definitive answer on it. However, for me, I interpret it as something I should do. I am a woman of deep faith. I believe that Jesus left heaven and came to earth, lived as a human, died, was resurrected, and now sits at the right hand of God. And the reason he says he did all that is so I can have life to the full. For me, that means I should do just that.

For me, spiritually, life to the full means examining everything. Getting all my questions answered—being like the people from Berea in the book of Acts—I am going to examine the Scriptures to see if what people are saying about who God is and what he has written is true. I'm not just going to take someone's word for it! I embrace, even celebrate, my spiritual curiosity. It deepens my faith. Part of that is also going and seeing the places that still stand today that are mentioned in the Bible. Are they real? What do they look like now? To date, I've been on seven guided biblical study tours, but I've also done research and studied places myself.

This also segues into how I use my leisure time to live life to the full. A long time ago, after receiving some sage advice from my father, I opted to pursue a career doing something I love. I have not regretted that, as it helps me in my full life. I also love to travel. After my mother passed away, I made a promise to her and to myself that I would never regret that I didn't do something I always wanted to do. I would make sure that I would find a way to do it, so I could live a full life on this earth and glorify God all at the same time. With that, I've taken numerous cruises, traveled to amazing sites both domestic and international, visited with friends far and wide, and tried food and drinks that I had to learn to pronounce, all while having the best time. Again, Jesus did not come for us to have a boring, mundane, run-of-the-mill life. He came so that we may have life and have it to the full...and I vow to always do just that.

Courtney Wacker's Testimony:
Emotional Health and Social Justice
—The Charlotte Church, North Carolina

Living life to the full has its challenges. I sometimes find myself wanting to perform for my parents and to be a people pleaser. What I have come to realize through spending time with Cresenda Jones is that I need to please God. I have a strong will to make sure my emotional health is taken care of.

Throughout my life, I have also found times when social justice issues are important to me. With the death of many Black and Brown individuals in the US due to police shootings, COVID, and hearing stories of what my friends and people of color go through every day in the United States, living life to the full means loving people as myself. I have had internships that allowed me to serve my community and encourage those who are different from me.

Being born with a hearing impairment and having hearing aids gives me the chance to be tied in to the deaf community and has also inspired me to learn Spanish. I hope to be an interpreter for both communities in the future, which will help me live my life to the full.

Peter Awolumate's Testimony:
Missions and Cultures
—Greater Philadelphia Church of Christ, New Jersey

The mindset of living life to the full was ignited in me later in my life—I think, if I recall, a year or two after I graduated from college. Before that, growing up, I always had a passion to travel and experience different cultures in different parts of the world. This hidden passion of mine was revealed when I watched a Bollywood movie called *Kuch Kuch Hota Hai* when I was eleven or twelve years of age. The Indian movie I watched sparked in me the curiosity to explore all other countries around the world that are rich in culture, like India.

Losing my father suddenly at a very young age, as well other people I loved and admired, made me realize that our lives are but a mist—life goes as quickly as it comes! Life is very short, and tomorrow is not promised, which is sad, but it is the truth. With that realization, I focused on living out my love of travel, and that is what I am currently doing and will continue to do. My passion for traveling and exploring different cultures has led me to desire being a full-time international missionary—as a single or married person—just like my role model in the faith, the Apostle Paul.

My first church missions trip, which is very dear to my heart, was to Kathmandu, Nepal. The trip really transformed me. I have also been to Lebanon—my first HOPE Singles serving trip. I can't wait to do many more missions and HOPE trips. Philippians 1:21 is my favorite scripture in the Bible: "For to me to live is Christ and to die is gain." I love this scripture so much because it encapsulates the mindset of Paul as he lived his passion to the full. I desire this scripture to be my motto as well as I continue to walk with God and continue to live life to the full!

Melika Miller's Testimony:
Dreaming and Trusting God
—The Memphis Church, Tennessee

Moving to New York was never in my mind in the beginning, but God allowed me to move there. I'm from rural Arkansas, so you can imagine the culture shock I experienced. Becoming a disciple in NYC and living there for twenty years was something I could not have dreamed of for myself. I have dreams like a lot of you do, but my dreams did not compare to the dreams God had for me before I was born. When I allowed myself to submit my dreams to him, I began to really live life to the fullest as Jesus said. I was holding on to this idea of what I imagined I could do, but like Ephesians 3:20 says, the Lord is able to do immeasurably more than all we ask or imagine!

But be careful what you ask for because it can come true! Be ready, and the Lord will make you ready when it is time. This is what he has done with my life. After moving to NYC, I had the chance to teach school, temp with different companies, work as a bookkeeper, do extra work for TV and film, and perform on different stages in the New York and New England area. I even had the chance to sing at the United Nations. But all this was part of my Father's big picture for my life, preparing me for what is to come. Each experience helped me to grow deeper in my faith and more in tune with his Spirit and his presence. He was training me on how to walk with his Spirit and see him in action in every part of my life. He taught me that my life is not my own. He allowed me to do all these things because he knows my nature and how I love an adventure, but in all of this, he wanted me to learn how to walk with him and not walk ahead of him or linger behind him. New York was my training ground for the things to come in my life.

In 2017, I was allowed to go to Cairo, Egypt. I cast lots for where he wanted me to go for vacation, and he chose Cairo. At that moment, I didn't know what he had in mind for me, but I was excited for the adventure ahead. I was in Cairo for a week, and during that time I saw all the things I had ever dreamed of seeing as a child and more. It was an amazing adventure, but in all of it I was looking for him, waiting for the Lord to reveal to me his reason for sending me on this trip. On our drive back from church one night, he did. Over the years, he has trained me to listen to his voice, to know his voice versus my voice or Satan's voice. This night on the drive back I heard him. He said, "You see how you are sitting in the cab with a driver whom you do not know, but you are relaxed in this seat believing he is going to take you where you need to be. You don't know the direction of where to go, but you trust that he is going to take you there safely. Why can't you do this with me, even though you know me? You have seen all the things you wanted to see and things you didn't even know you wanted to see because I know you. Trust me and relax in me." This was a tangible way of him showing me where my life was about to go and how much I needed to trust him.

In 2018, he told me after twenty years of living in NYC that it was time for me to go. I was scared and didn't know where he wanted me to go, but I knew I had to prepare to leave. I was about to graduate from Fordham University with my master's in pastoral counseling and spiritual care (which was a part of the Lord's plan too), but I didn't know what I was going to do next. He began to shut the doors in NYC, and I was forced to move. He revealed that he wanted me to move to Memphis, Tennessee so that I could be closer to my family.

Moving to Memphis at the time was not my choice, and I couldn't understand why he did it, but looking back over my life I can see the puzzle he is piecing together. I am living the dream God dreamed for me before I was born. I am walking into the purpose he wrote out for my life before I even existed. He is teaching me what it means to trust him in the unknown and he will lead me to places I have always wanted to see and those I have never imagined I would. One of my favorite quotes is "Life is a journey. Enjoy it." My life has definitely been a journey, full of adventures written by our Father. He is an amazing Author and I'm so excited to see where this next chapter lands me!

Michele Smith's Testimony:
The Value of Being Intentional
—Northview Church of Christ, Georgia

As a single, it can be easy to get lost in the mix of couples and families. For many years I was a single mom. I still am, but now my children are grown. When they were younger, I spent most of my time with families in order to get the parenting support I needed, and I didn't really fit in with the singles. When the kids were older, I had to find a space where I felt connected. While it might be nice if those connections just happened automatically, I found the best connections happened when I was intentional about meeting people, spending time getting to know them, and being vulnerable enough for them to know me.

I am almost as social as I would like to be. I say almost, because I'm not very good at initiating social activities even though I really enjoy them. Sometimes it's even hard for me to get out to something I've decided to do (go to a concert with friends, for example) but once I get there, I have a wonderful time. The limiting factor here is me, not the absence of opportunity!

I have amazing friends and consider myself very wealthy in this regard. I love the balance they provide—some help me with my social gaps, some hear my heart and support me, and others love me no matter what and provide wise counsel. This is another value of being intentional and seeking those relationships that help me be my best self.

I really feel life "to the full" when I am intentional about the process of my Bible study and prayer time. It can be easy to do a "drive-thru" version of time with God. While this meets my basic needs, it does not promote improvement or health. I love the peace that comes when feeling like I am walking my life path with my loving Creator God and his Son, Jesus.

Ivette Brito's Testimony:
"Do It Afraid"
—Northview Church of Christ, Georgia

I have always loved the outdoors. Being out in nature has always made me feel close to God. Hiking is one of my favorite things to do. For the last several years a few sisters and I have planned a yearly hiking or backpacking trip. The year I turned fifty was our first group trip together. We hiked the Grand Canyon rim to rim, and it was amazing. The trip was not without its challenges. We woke up every morning before sunrise to get ready for our hike and have quiet times. On our second day I had an accident, in which I fell while trying to step up on a bridge and almost rolled off the bridge. One of the sisters was able to quickly grab me by my heavy backpack to keep me from falling. As frightening as that was, it was even more scary to go back up the Canyon the next day. After the fall, walking on some of the narrow ledges was terrifying for me. I prayed to God as we walked. When I wasn't praying, I was singing, "Holy Father grant me peace." And God did! Although there was fear at times, there was also peace knowing that God was with us.

The following summer our hiking trip was planned in South Dakota. On our second hike to Black Elk Peak, as we were reaching the top, I began to feel terrible. It was difficult to walk uphill, and I felt lightheaded. I thought that I might have been dehydrated or that my autoimmune disorder was acting up. On the way down, I felt that I was going to pass out. I prayed, "God, whatever this is, please don't let me die up here!" When we made it back to the parking lot, a park ranger showed up. The ranger overrode my refusal of an ambulance and told one friend that I looked like he did when he had his heart attack. I was actually having a heart attack and did not know it! I later found out that the rangers don't patrol that area very much. If that ranger had not been there and had not known the signs of a heart attack, I probably wouldn't be here today. To this day I believe he is my angel sent by God.

I once read this phrase: "Do it afraid." It has always stayed with me. Despite my fall in the Canyon and my heart attack in South Dakota, I choose not to allow fear to take away living my best life for God and with God. I can't say that I don't have concerns about what could happen when I go hiking. But I pray and then I "do it afraid." Last summer we all went to Alaska and did a couple of hikes out there. Other than the rain on our camping night in Denali, there were no mishaps or incidents. It was an amazing trip!

Spiritually, I work to rely on God in everything I do. I consistently pray throughout my day, even about trivial things. I trust that God is with me in the good and in the challenging times. With my relationships, I often think of how Jesus would treat that person and try my best to follow in his steps.

Danial Naqashi's Testimony: Journey with Jesus
—Valley Christian, Las Vegas, Nevada

As I've navigated my life as a disciple of Jesus, my aim has been to develop my relationship with him and glorify him. In a journey of hills and valleys, I have learned that no matter how hard I try, I will never be able to control my circumstances. I know that God has given me freedom of choice, which allows me some control in my personal life. However, I also realize that to pursue control of anything beyond that would only achieve an illusion of control. I decided to no longer base my faith, joy, happiness, spiritual well-being, or mental well-being on something as fickle as my circumstances. I choose instead to look to God and shift my trust completely to him, having confidence that he is the only One with ultimate control.

Throughout the many challenges I've faced in my life, I've gradually discovered my desperate need for God. From him flow the only streams of living water, which can quench my soul, while everything else in this world is an empty cistern, promising water but dry as dirt.

In John 15, Jesus paints an image of a plant, with him as the vine and us (his disciples) as the branches. I was once a branch that connected to God as though he were a charging station, connecting only to fill up enough to get through the day, then off I went. What happens if a branch does not remain in the vine? It withers and eventually dies. I've learned that it is the same for us: if we are not drawing our strength from Jesus, we are relying on our own finite supply. Experience has shown me that my own strength is not sufficient to live a fruitful, godly life. We need to always be connected to Jesus, because he is our source of spiritual nourishment. The courage to live and lead boldly for God doesn't come from us, but rather flows from a place of closeness to him.

When we understand how great our God is (to the extent that we are able), we see that our problems are minuscule by comparison. When we stop trying to control our circumstances, letting them define us, we are free to ground ourselves in Jesus. Being rooted in Jesus, we can receive the spiritual nourishment we need to not only survive, but be fruitful in serving God.

Irene Umaña Lindo's Testimony:
Loss and Continued Service
—Iglesia Internacional de Cristo, Costa Rica

I was baptized and received my salvation more than thirty-six years ago. When I first gave my life to Christ, I had no idea what that would entail over the decades. Today, I am accepting that this journey to heaven is not easy, and I know that I cannot do it without God by my side.

I have had my highs and lows throughout the years. In my lows, I lost my husband, my parents, and my two aunts. These two aunts had cared for me while I was living in the United States. Most recently, I got ill. As a result, I am now taking high doses of a medication that causes easily noticeable adverse reactions. I have been told that I will need to take the medication for the rest of my life.

After much prayer, God opened my eyes and my heart regarding my illness. I began to understand that being ill helps me to draw closer to him so that I can make it to heaven. God's love has been confusing at times because it is not necessarily based on me being healthy or not having losses in my life. God's plan is simply to help me to make it to heaven. 2 Corinthians 4:18 is my favorite scripture that I hold onto: "So we fix our eyes not on what is seen, but on what is unseen, since what is seen is temporary, but what is unseen is eternal."

Despite my health challenges, I continue to serve in my church fellowship. I serve on our church *HOPE worldwide* committee, serve others, contribute to our mature women's group, and was recently asked to share for communion. I pray that God continues to be glorified in my life.

Wendy Walker-Drakes' Testimony:
Enjoying a Second Spring
—Bridgetown Church of Christ, Barbados

I am a Jamaican-born woman who has been a disciple for thirty-five years, and I've lived for the last thirty in Barbados. During the various seasons of my life, I have negotiated pitfalls and schemes. I am grateful to God for all he does as he shows us how to access and to live a powerful single life. As a woman who was married and is now single, I am now reaping the rewards of enjoying this second season, this second spring—it is a privileged life.

To see the Holy Spirit move, to experience the attributes of God with intimacy, having accepted that God is my husband and friend (Isaiah 54:4–5), is living life with eyes wide open. It isn't always sweet or easy as we learn to strip off the dependence on self. I have shifted from the attitude of "I got this" and moved to a place of "Who got this? My Jesus!" as my Trinidadian brother and artist, Rizon, has declared lyrically.

This requires wading through God's word and being able to see him come through with his answers to situations, accepting that he knows what's best. That's hard for an independent overachiever in this world. I'm learning that the kingdom of God is very different and how to love walking in the Way.

Thank you, God, for teaching me and for loving me...all of single me.

Dana Wynne's Testimony:
From Basketball to God
—Valley Christian, Las Vegas, Nevada

As a girl born and raised in the inner city in New Jersey, there were many directions my life could have gone, but God gave me a passion for basketball that saved my life. I was "married" to basketball for thirty-two years. Everything I did was to protect my relationship with my husband (basketball), and this attitude had damaging effects  on my life that were not apparent until I studied the Bible and got baptized at the age of thirty-two. At that time, I realized that my relationship with God was the priority, and that basketball had been his tool to get me closer to him.

Now, at forty-seven years old, I am a happy single woman living every day to serve in my ministry. God has blessed me in many ways. Since I was totally committed to basketball for so long, I never wanted to be married. That has been a tremendous blessing because I am able to serve in many more ways. It can be a battle to avoid giving in to my sinful, independent nature of being with "me, myself and I," but God has helped me by surrounding me with amazing sisters and brothers. I sometimes wonder if I'll be lonely as I get older, but being with God as my husband (Isaiah 54:5) on this journey, I believe I can continue to live life to the full.

Conclusion

Through this book, I hope that you have been encouraged by God, his plan for our lives (John 10:10), my story, the power of our minds, the possibility of our impact, God's grace, God's intimate guidance, and the inspiring testimonies. Despite one of the greatest disappointments in my life (the ending of a relationship), I am determined to walk with God and trust him on my journey. I am determined to live life to the full now! I will continue to work at learning from the events in my life. I will continue to do all I can to use my messes and tests as messages and testimonies! I pray that we see each other at the "Great Banquet" (Luke 14)!

> *Therefore, my dear brothers and sisters, stand firm. Let nothing move you. Always give yourselves fully to the work of the Lord, because you know that your labor in the Lord is not in vain.* (1 Corinthians 15:58)

Praise to God for a Living Hope

> *Praise be to the God and Father of our Lord Jesus Christ! In his great mercy he has given us new birth into a living hope through the resurrection of Jesus Christ from the dead, and into an inheritance that can never perish, spoil or fade. This inheritance is kept in heaven for you, who through faith are shielded by God's power until the coming of the salvation that is ready to be revealed in the last time. In all this you greatly rejoice, though now for a little while you may have had to suffer grief in all kinds of trials. These have come so that the proven genuineness of your faith—of greater worth than gold, which perishes even though refined by fire—may result in praise, glory and honor when Jesus Christ is revealed. Though you have not seen him, you love him; and even though you do not see him now, you believe in him and are filled with an inexpressible and glorious joy, for you are receiving the end result of your faith, the salvation of your souls.* (1 Peter 1:3–9)

Keys to An Achievable Outcome

And the LORD answered me: "Write the vision; make it plain on tablets, so that it can be read on the run. For still the vision awaits its appointed time; it points to the end; aches for the coming—it will not lie. If it seems slow, wait for it; it will surely come; it will come right on time." (Habakkuk 2:2–3 ESV and MSG combined)

Now to him who is able to do far more abundantly beyond all that we ask or think, according to the power that works within us, to him be the glory in the church and in Christ Jesus to all generations forever and ever. Amen. (Ephesians 3:20–21 NASB)

Forgetting what lies behind and straining forward to what lies ahead, I press on toward the goal for the prize of the upward call of God in Christ Jesus. (Philippians 3:13–14 ESV)

How is it possible that I don't have it now?

1. Stated in the positive.

What specifically do I want? *Philippians 4:8*

2. Specify present situation.

Where am I now? *Romans 12:3*

3. Specify outcome.

What will I see, hear, feel, etc., when I have it?

As if now. Make compelling. Insert in future ((Time Line Therapy@ Creating Your Future@ technique). *Mark 11:22–24; Proverbs 18:21; Matthew 21:22; 2 Corinthians 4:13; Hebrews 11; Proverbs 29:18; Isaiah 43:19*

4. Specify evidence procedure.

How will I know when I have it? *Proverbs 21:5*

5. Is it congruently desirable?

What will this outcome get for me or allow me to do? *Jeremiah 29:11; Proverbs 3:6*

6. Is it self-initiated and self-maintained?

Is it only for me? *Colossians 3:2*

7. Is it appropriately contextualized?

Where, when, how, and with whom do I want it? *1 Corinthians 12:12–27*

8. What resources are needed?

What do I have now and what do I need in order to get my outcome? *Isaiah 40:31; Jeremiah 17:7; Matthew 6:33; Matthew 19:26; Matthew 21:22; Romans 8:28*

Have I ever had or done this before?

Do I know anyone who has?

Can I act as if I have it?

9. Is it ecological?

For what purpose do I want this?

What will I gain or lose if I have it?

What will happen if I get it?

What won't happen if I get it?

What will happen if I don't get it?

What won't happen if I don't get it? *Isaiah 32:8; John 4:34; Romans 12:2*

So do not throw away your confidence; it will be richly rewarded. You need to persevere so that when you have done the will of God, you will receive what he has promised. (Hebrews 10:35–36)

Adapted from Tad James Co., LLC (2018). Time Line Therapy® Practitioner Training Manual.

Bibliography

DePaulo, Bella (2022). The Number-One Reason Singles Aren't Looking for Relationships. *Psychology Today.* Retrieved from: https://www.psychologytoday.com/us/blog/living-single/202204/the-number-one-reason-singles-arent-looking-relationships

Dispenza, Joe (2017). *Breaking the Habit of Being Yourself: How to Lose Your Mind and Create a New One.* New York, NY: Hay House Publishers.

Dispenza, Joe (n.d.) Video retrieved from: https://www.instagram.com/reel/Cc2wajBP6er/?utm_source=ig_web_copy_link

James, Tad and Adriana (2009). *The Secret of Creating Your Future.* United States: Tad James Co.

James, T. (n.d.). NLP Communication Model. Retrieved from: www.nlpcoaching.com/nlp-a-model-of-communication-and-personality/

Jones, Cresenda (2014). *Spiritual Maturity: God's Will for Emotional Health and Healing.* Boca Raton, FL: Joy Publishing.

Jones, Cresenda (2021). *Spiritual Transformation: Emotional Intelligence and Freedom.* Spring, TX: Illumination Publishers.

Mann, Sonya (n.d.). Tony Robbins Says Success Is Only 20 Percent Skill—And the Rest Is All in Your Head. Retrieved from: https://www.inc.com/sonya-mann/tony-robbins-says-entrepreneurship-is-not-for-everyone.html

Robbins, Tony (n.d.). The Influential Power of Meta-Programs: How to Use Meta-Programs to Increase your Influence. Retrieved from: https://www.tonyrobbins.com/stories/leadership-academy/influential-power-meta-programs/

Seamands, David A., and Beth Funk (1992). *Healing for Damaged Emotions Workbook.* Colorado: SP Publications.

Tad James Co., LLC (2018). Master Time Line Therapy® Practitioner Training Manual.

Tad James Co., LLC (2018). Time Line Therapy® Practitioner Training Manual.

Wikipedia (n.d.). Locus of control. Retrieved from: https://en.wikipedia.org/wiki/Locus_of_control

Wikipedia (n.d.). Meditation. Retrieved from: https://en.wikipedia.org/wiki/Meditation#cite_note-FOOTNOTEWalshShapiro2006228%E2%80%93229-1

Additional Books by Cresenda Jones
available at www.ipibooks.com

Spiritual Maturity: God's Will for Emotional Health and Healing

Without emotional intelligence and personal growth, our lives will be like the seed that fell among thorns (Luke 8:14). We will not be able to most effectively or spiritually handle life's worries, riches, and pleasures, and we will not mature. This book addresses issues that we must consider in order to live as emotionally, spiritually, and relationally mature adults. Not a quick-read book, it contains scriptures to contemplate, personal sharing, paradigm-changing insights, and reflection questions.

Chapters:
1. What You Don't Know Will Hurt You
2. My Emotional Health and Healing Journey
3. You Are Not Alone: The Power of Healing Discussion Groups
4. My Personal Heroes: Courage and Healing
5. Spiritual Foundation
6. Dig a Little Deeper: Wisdom and Emotional Health
7. Numbing the Pain and Repeating the Cycle
8. Our Fathers
9. How to Change: More than Just a Decision
Epilogue: Still a Work in Progress
Appendix I: Mental Health Disorders
Appendix II: When to See a Professional
Appendix III: Additional Change Models

Spiritual Transformation: Emotional Intelligence and Freedom

In a world in which interpersonal relationships have become increasingly depersonalized due to social media, the ability to identify and manage one's own emotions (as well as the emotions of others) is becoming a lost skill. This skill, known as emotional intelligence (EI), is an essential tool for disciples of Jesus, who have been tasked by God to appeal to the hearts and souls of others, in an effort to win them over and share the good news of salvation. Like other aptitudes, EI falls on a normal curve: some people have a great deal of natural EI, and others have less. Fortunately, EI can be understood, learned, and developed. In her book, Cresenda guides the reader to a better understanding of the theory and science of EI, while also providing very practical, Bible-based exercises to improve EI and progress toward greater spiritual, social, and emotional maturity. A must-have book for anyone who deals with people, which is pretty much everyone!

—Michael S. Shapiro, PhD, author of *Rejoice Always*

Chapters:
1. Take the *Emotional Intelligence 2.0* Test—Assessment Is Imperative!
2. Life without EQ
3. What is Emotional Intelligence?
4. Master Your Mind
5. The Cost of Repressing Emotions
6. God, Emotions, and Emotional Intelligence
7. The Bible on the Four Core EQ skills
8. Build Your EQ skills – The Bible on Emotional Intelligence 2.0's 66 Strategies
9. Time Line Therapy® – Transforming Our Neurology
10. Three Requisites for Mind Changes and Soul Transformations
Appendix: Is There Anything Helpful Outside God's Word?

www.ingramcontent.com/pod-product-compliance
Lightning Source LLC
Chambersburg PA
CBHW021647120626
46545CB00002B/740